# LIVING
# STRESS
# F



## AN INTROD ION TO THE "HOW" OF LIVING GOD'S WAY

## NO FEAR
## NO WORRY
## NO STRESS

*Ron Davies*

ISBN 09536760 0 5

British Library Cataloguing in Publication Data
A catalogue record for this book is available from the British Library.

Published by
Joel Publishing Ltd.
P.O.Box 283
Margate
CT9 3GW

Printed by
Martell Press Ltd
Hopes Lane
Ramsgate
Kent
CT12 6UW

## ACKNOWLEDGEMENTS

Scripture Verses Quoted and Listed themes are from various Bible Translations as follows:-

Verses taken from The Living Bible © 1971 are used by permission of Kingsway Publications, Eastbourne, Sussex BN21 3UN.

Scripture taken from the Amplified(R) New Testament © Copyright The Lockman Foundation 1954,1958,1987. Used by permission. Scripture taken from the Amplified Bible, Old Testament. Copyright © 1965, 1987 by the Zondervan Corporation. Used by permission.

Scripture quotations from THE MESSAGE. Copyright © 1993, 1994,1995. Used by permission of NavPress Publishing Group.

Scripture quotations taken from The Holy Bible, New International Version Copyright © 1973, 1978, 1984 by New York International Bible Society. Used by permission of Hodder & Stoughton Limited. All rights reserved.

Scripture taken from The New King James Version Bible. Copyright © 1982 by Thomas Nelson, Inc. Used by permission. All rights reserved.

Special thanks to my precious family and many friends from whom I received constant encouragement, critical appraisals, suggestions and commendations. To them I owe so much in producing this book. Special thanks too to Colin Urquhart for his foreword and to Christo Beukes for the cover design.

# LIVING STRESS FREE

**"A CALM AND UNDISTURBED MIND AND HEART ARE THE LIFE AND HEALTH OF THE BODY"**
**(Proverbs 14:30 AMP)**

**This book is dedicated to all who have been robbed of carefree living, their rightful inheritance in Christ Jesus.**

# LIVING STRESS FREE

## INDEX

# LIVING STRESS FREE

## FOREWORD

When you read a Foreword you want to know whether the rest of the book is worth reading. Well, this one most definitely is, and I cannot recommend it highly enough.

Here Ron Davies introduces the reader in a clear way to the principles of faith in God's grace and goodness. When you live by these principles you experience the flow of God's blessing and provision for every area of your life.

Life is too short to read theoretical books. Ron, together with his wife, Dorothy, has a long history of having to trust God "in the field". His faithful ministry is an expression of the scriptural principle to which Paul refers when he says: "The only thing that matters is faith expressing itself in love".

Ron Davies shows how the principles of practical and dynamic faith are worked out in a relationship of love for Jesus and for those He died to save. He keeps to the essential simplicity of the gospel and shows how these truths will have a practical impact on any who seek to live in the good of God's Word in the power of the Holy Spirit.

Jesus says that the truth will set you free. This book is an exposition of truth that can set the reader free from negative thought patterns and misunderstandings that have had a ruinous effect on their lives, or have simply prevented them from knowing God's best for them: fullness of life in Christ.

Of course, to live a happy, fulfilled life, you will need to put these principles into operation. This book will not only encourage you to do this, but will also demonstrate that such a life is within reach of every born-again believer who wants to live stress free. The message is clear: this is what you need to do; this is how to do it and **you** are able to do it through the grace of God.

I trust this book will lead you into a life of trusting God in a new way, and realising you can cast all your cares on Him, that He will carry the load. He will even carry you!

Colin Urquhart
Kingdom Faith Ministries
Foundry Road
Horsham
West Sussex RH13 5PX
U.K.

## PREFACE

Do you want to be happy?

By "happy" I mean living carefree in God's care all the time and really enjoying life to the full. This fulfilling lifestyle covers all situations including times of being intensely busy. However, even when busy, enjoying a life where frustration, fear and anxiety cannot gain an entrance, where stress too is absent. In response to this you might say "impossible!" but faith-evidence based on Bible narrative says otherwise.

Our Shepherd-Saviour God never drives, always leads. Where does He lead? According to the World's favourite Psalm, our Good-Shepherd God always leads into peace and rest, both of which are to be enjoyed along the pathway to the prize(1). King David's life from shepherding sheep to leading Israel was a tumultuous pathway. Amidst family jealousy, being hunted as a fugitive, countering betrayal, fighting battles, quelling rebellion plus great personal failures, he learned the secret of living God's way. In Psalm 23 David challenges us to find the secret too.

Happiness—-carefree living is God's will for you. That is why, in spite of past disappointments, current life-pressures and demanding work-loads, carefree living is within your reach. The big question is this. Have you the humility to admit that, somewhere in your Christian experience, you've been conned into accepting your present 'up and down' life-style as permanent and are you prepared for God to change it for something infinitely better? If your reply is an emphatic **"yes!"**, then this book will assist you in discovering for yourself God's wisdom, His ***"..ways of pleasantness ...paths of peace" (Proverbs 3:17 New King James Bible).*** The journey into His peace results in an enjoyable, progressive life-style that eventually will eliminate all stress out of living.

All the various aspects of truth shared in these pages are far from being a glib recipe, a quick-fix formula for instant success but rather a progressive experience of growing-up into Jesus or an unfolding of a way (the 'narrow way' perhaps?). The pace of progress is up to you depending on whether you travel in the fast or slow lane. Either lane makes for a steady advance into stress free living in this hostile world, God's plan for all His children. Under the Holy Spirit's guidance you are tutored as a King's kid to discover the secret of living by the faith of Jesus Christ who died to give you an inheritance in Himself (2).

Kingdom-living is an adventure in possessing the substance of what was bequeathed you when

Jesus was crucified. That inheritance includes stress free living. He now expects you (and all born-again believers) to lay hold of His gift and to experience it for yourself. Not as something that on random occasions comes and then is lost but as a permanent part of the structure of your life in Christ.

At this point conclusions should not be drawn that, up front, there is nothing but calm seas and blue skies awaiting you. Like everyone else, life's pleasant occasions give way, from time to time, to difficult situations including adversity and sorrow. However, the good news is that, in learning to live God's stress free way, there is secured to you a developing ability to cope with anything that could possibly arise to faze your peace of mind and tranquillity of spirit. There are so many Scriptures that point to this fact and they remove any doubt that God earnestly desires His children to fully enjoy His glorious gift of life. Jesus described it as abundant (3), in reality—living stress free.

Every truth highlighted in this book has been personally walked out over many years under all manner of circumstances, conditions and cultures. These have covered single and married life, bringing up children, industry (shop floor & management), full-time Christian ministry both in Britain, and abroad in countries where civil war has raged with devastating results.

The writer continues to press forward to gain more of this promised abundant life and would encourage you to do the same. The sheer enjoyment of revealed truth personally applied, will bring with it a corresponding release into God's peace and this in turn increases hunger for more.

Perhaps the best description of learning to live stress free is 'sampling heaven on the way to heaven'. Wouldn't you like to do the same? The moment you start, beneficial results will follow.

**Bible References.**

---

1. **John 16:33, Philippians 4:6-7, Psalm 23. New King James Bible.**
2. **Galatians 2:20, Romans 1:17, 1Peter 1:3-5. Amplified New Testament.**
3. **John 10:10 Amplified New Testament.**

## RESOURCE GUIDE

All Scripture quotes are in *'Italics'*. Numbers in brackets indicate Bible references that source stated truth and are found at the end of each chapter. Bracketed letters indicate the source of quotes etc. and are listed at the back of the book in alphabetical order. Please don't ignore any of the Bible references but check them all until understanding is birthed in your heart concerning each truth under the spotlight.

Perhaps the best way of doing this is to read each chapter through, and afterwards to look up the references. Each should be considered with a re-reading of the chapter if necessary, until your heart is anchored in the particular truth presented. You will also find it helpful to compare the given Scripture portions using different Bible versions. Each version will complement the others and so broaden understanding of the truth under consideration. **Always remember that God caused all Scripture to be written for your benefit(4). That fact makes you the subject when researching truth, no matter what truth is in focus.**

The whole of the Bible is a divine revelation of our Lord Jesus Christ and, through Him, the knowledge of our Father-God. The written word finds its consummation in the Living Word, Jesus Christ. The Father now speaks to you, to us all, through His only begotten and beloved Son, Jesus Christ. His motivation for doing this is His love for us. When Christ died and rose again, He made it possible for us, for you, to have a relationship with His Father through Him.

This becomes reality as in faith there is an acceptance of Christ's atoning death on the Cross for your sins, your selfishness, your rebellion. When Christ ascended as the all-conquering Redeemer, the Father both exalted Him and gave the Holy Spirit to Him to give to every Believer. Through and by the Holy Spirit several aspects of truth concerning the divinity of Jesus Christ are revealed,

1. As Creator of all things.

2. His Incarnation and life among us.

3. His supreme sacrifice at the Cross for us.

4. His resurrection and glorious Ascension to the throne of God where He now reigns supreme.

5. As God-Man living in the hearts of all who by faith have made Him their Saviour.

This five part sublime disclosure makes us realise that we are in Him and He in us. Our God never sleeps or takes a holiday. His presence with us is constant at all times. He plans in love for our well being.

The truth highlighted in this book assumes your belief in these foundational revelations. The Father now speaks in the person of His Son, Who is declared to be the 'Living Word' (5). He, Jesus, is discovered in the written word, the Bible, by the Holy Spirit. Your embrace of truth, as it is revealed, ultimately establishes your spiritual identity which is vital to Stress Free Living.

**Bible References.**

**4. 2 Timothy 3:16-17 Amplified New Testament.**
**5. John 1:1-2 & 14, Hebrews 1:1-3. Amplified New Testament.**

# CHAPTER ONE

## BELIEVING BEGETS ACTION

[illegible] Jesus constantly challenges us to **believe** [illegible] Him and I'm sure you would say, you do. [illegible] wo simple questions and your answers to [illegible] t well mean a re-think of what it means to [illegible] d 'follow' the Lord.

**[illegible] 1. Are you 'on top' of your [illegible] ces (in victory) all of the time? Y[illegible]**

**Q[illegible] 2. Do you believe that Jesus is the S[illegible] Yes or No?**

Sh[illegible] nswers be **no** to Q.1 and **yes** to Q.2, the[illegible] arises because your answers are at va[illegible] he Scripture that says, ***"Who is it tha[illegible] us over (that conquers) the world bu[illegible] elieves that Jesus is the Son of Go[illegible]*** **5:5 Amplified New Testament).** Acc[illegible] to this Scripture both of your answers should have been 'yes'. If they were otherwise, then you will need to hold yourself ready to re-think the matter of 'believing'. In this instance, that Jesus is the Son of God, and possibly other subjects as they are raised in this book.

Our Lord Jesus said,

**"IF THE WORLD IS ON YOUR BACK,YOU'VE GOT BURDENS. COME, WALK WITH ME AND I'LL TEACH YOU HOW TO LIVE A BETTER WAY. I PROMISE YOU IT'S EASY TO LEARN, EASY TO LIVE AND THERE ARE NO HEAVY BURDENS."**
**(Personal paraphrase of Matthew 11:28)**

Long ago this promise gripped me. I grasped the truth that God was offering me life to the full if I would 'believe' and 'follow' the Unchanging One. My 'believing' and 'following' has undergone many adjustments since taking up the offer and no doubt more will come as faith's pathway unfolds.

Every Olympic athlete has in their mind the supreme prize — a gold medal. God offers a far greater and much more worthwhile prize, the incredible 'Crown of Life' (6), to all who believe and follow Him. You may have experienced already something of God's goodness but the best still awaits you as you apply yourself to the simple task of acquiring and enjoying it, or should I say Him, for **Jesus is your life** (7).

You only have one life to live with no chance of a second time round. However, opportunity came your way when the Lord of Glory entered your life, eradicated your past and gave you a new destiny. Every obstacle to you maximising on life has been removed including the ability to get rid of junk luggage. Jesus made it perfectly clear when chatting to His own disciples and a gathered crowd that carrying fears, anxious thoughts and stress accomplishes nothing positive but actually detracts from Life. It being better to jettison such junk (8). ***"Give your burdens to the Lord, He will carry them" (Psalm 55:22 Living Bible)***. This verse plus others make it obvious that God intends and plans for human life to be lived burden-free.

God's sacrificial love has procured everything you need for living His way (9). Whatever threatens, in Christ you win (10). At the outset of your new life in Jesus your faith in Him planted your feet on the road to freedom and all was well. However, your present situation may suggest that despite a good beginning the pace and pressure of everyday life has gradually given you unwanted burdens and you have been at a loss to know how to lose them. Over an extended time the overall accrued result is that anxiety, fear and stress have gained access into your life and largely excluded peace and joy.

God's ordered destiny for every one is not to endure a sub-standard life of fluctuating emotions but rather to enjoy a daily victory parade (11). As captain of your salvation Christ leads you each day to gather the rewards of victory. Not the least of these rewards is His peace that embraces and establishes wholeness, health and well-being in every area of life without exception. Your response to this could well be, " that's OK when all is well but what about my negative circumstances? " It is true that often one's circumstances may give rise to unpleasant situations but when these occur it is God's intention to turn those negatives into positives.

Much of God's goodness is completely missed when we fight our circumstances with aggressive prayer in which the enemy is rebuked with intense emotion, or, on the other hand passively accept whatever comes without question. God invites us to bring Him into every situation regardless of it being favourable or otherwise (12).

Life in Jesus is not intended to fluctuate from being up one moment and down the next, with our circumstances dictating the flow of our feelings. Rather it should be a level, super highway to heaven with our emotions stabilised by truth and fully under God's control. With Him in the driving seat of our lives, all our circumstances can actually work good for us. He who created and sustains this giant universe is well able to guide us out of our comparatively small problems into His solutions.

Life that Jesus gives is saturated with God's goodness and favour. All hindrances have been removed for 'heaven on earth' to be realised. The substance of His many promises are for us to have, hold and enjoy here and now. These exceedingly great and precious promises are given in order to lead us into carefree living (13). Stress, fear, worry and such burdens have no place in God's purposes for His children. Everyone owes it to God, to others, and to themselves to move forward into His promised, faith-filled, burden-free life.

In living such a life the emphasise is not on you doing anything other than simply believing truth as it's revealed. Without any conscious effort truth believed will affect your behaviour. For instance, if you believe that another person's property is theirs and theirs alone you will never resort to theft. Should you find something not yours, you'll take it to the Police to assist in restoring the lost property to its owner. Similarly, if you believe that cigarette smoking is injurious to health, you will not only refrain from the habit yourself but also choose non-smoking areas in public places. The action taken in both these examples is a direct result of belief.

Truth believed always has a powerful, liberating effect upon your life. ***"Jesus said, If you abide in My Word — hold fast to My teachings and live in accordance with them — you are truly My***

***disciples. And you will know the truth, and the truth will set you free."(John 8:31-32 Amplified New Testament).*** Belief in Jesus' words will create a desire for ever increasing freedom from those things that hinder your life in Christ and motivate you to read more and more of the Bible. The whole happy exercise promoting Christ-likeness in you.

During this time you will come to realise:-
1. All that God has in store for you — **unlimited provision.**
2. His high estimation of you — **unlimited consideration.**
3. All He has done for you, is doing and going to do— **unlimited love.**

Truth actively at work in your life will increase your understanding of God and this will bring you closer to Him. Obviously the more truth that becomes a part of you, the more enjoyable will be your daily walk with God. The main characteristic of this walk will be a developing recognition of His presence with you regardless of where you are and what you are doing. A natural progression from any daily 'quiet time' you may hold with God.

Elisabeth Fry, the 19th century reformer, said on her deathbed, "Since my heart was touched (by God), at the age of seventeen, I believe I have never awakened from sleep, in sickness or in health, by day or by night, without my first waking thought being how best I might serve the Lord"(A).

Andrew Murray (1828-1917), whose ministry sparked a revival in South Africa's then Cape Colony said, "to know God, to see God in everything and everywhere, in our daily life to be conscious of His presence so that we always walk with Him—-this is the true nobility of man; this is the life that faith lives. Faith can walk with God" (B) (C).

The fruit of a developing awareness of God's presence being always with you and for you is increased confidence. As you more and more realise His availability so the more your trust will grow. Each positive faith-response to Him being there with you will of necessity lead to much easier dialogue. Especially when you remember that, ***"In Him lie hidden all the mighty, untapped treasures of wisdom and knowledge" (Colossians 2:3 Living Bible).***

Travelling hand in hand with the Living One becomes a daily, ever increasing intimate adventure. In this 'premier league' you soon discover what it is to be 'more than a Conqueror'(14). You will find that being 'on top' of your circumstances is not life in a dream- world but the substance of an ongoing faith-experience called, victorious Christian living. As your feet continue to walk the road of simplicity, each faith-experience will challenge you to find another, and then another, and so on. All this ensures a regular advance into carefree living.

*** The life God gives to all who believe is filled with His presence and promises. This is settled in heaven and on earth. Only unbelief excludes them.**

*** Faith began your relationship with God. Only a continuing faith-walk will deepen it and develop maturity in you to the mutual delight of you both.**

*** It is from within that change first takes place when faith brings outlook and attitudes into harmony with God's purposes.** ***"It is God who works in you both to will and to do for His good pleasure" ( Philippians 2: 12-13 New King James Bible).***

**Bible References.**

---

6. **James 1:12, Revelation 3:11 Amplified New Testament.**
7. **1 John 5:11-13, Colossians 3:4 Amplified New Testament.**

8. Matthew 6:25-34 Amplified New Testament.
9. 2 Peter 1:3, Romans 8:32 Amplified New Testament.
10. Romans 5:17-21 The Message, page 371-372.
11. 2 Corinthians 2: 14-17 Amplified New Testament.
12. Proverbs 3:6 New International Version Bible.
13. 2 Peter 1:1-4 Amplified New Testament.
14. Romans 8:34-39 Amplified New Testament.

# CHAPTER TWO

## LET SENSE BE DUMB

Locked up in your heart there is an in built desire to please God, the outcome of the 'Will' of Jesus becoming effective in your life (15). However, the coming of this divine deposit can be short-circuited by human subtlety. There is always the possibility that, in wanting to please God, you can easily forget that His gift of Life in Christ is absolutely free and frustrate His grace by striving to earn His favour with sacrificial gifts of service. God's gift of Salvation is complete, it cannot be earned or bought by any personal sacrifice. Such works do not produce faith but hinder it. Genuine works of faith are those initiated and carried out by the individual Christian in loving obedience to the Holy Spirit's prompting and guidance.

Another great danger is the ease in which we can presume to know what God requires of us and then to go about it with great religious zeal. A parallel is to be found in those who constituted the Sardis Church who were described as being dead because God's word was being ignored in favour of their assumptions. They had busy but empty lives, a very sad story (16). It is so easy to mistake human wisdom and resources for the divine and move into action. All assumptions, if not recognised and dealt with, will eventually produce stress leading to possible breakdown.

The risen Christ is the role model for living God's way. Follow Him for success. The "how" of living to please God is given only to those who presume nothing but constantly search the Scriptures for answers. The importance of this is beyond measure endorsed by:- ***"Oh! the joys of those who ........ delight in doing everything God wants them to, and day and night are always meditating on His laws and thinking about ways to follow Him more closely. They are like trees along a river bank bearing luscious fruit each season without fail. Their leaves shall never wither, and all they do shall prosper. But for sinners, what a different story." (Psalm 1: 1-4 Living Bible)***

Only those who live according to the measure of God's Word personally revealed to them by the Spirit, can enjoy a never failing prosperity in life. These are they, who, being not satisfied with the truth they have and practice, are always seeking for more. Their focus in life being to please God in everything and in so doing find themselves constantly enriched. An enrichment of life, both natural and spiritual, that will also affect other lives. God blesses His children in order for them to be a channel of blessing, a fragrance of Christ, to others.

***"Without faith it is impossible to please God" (Hebrews 11:6 New King James Bible)*** Whatever your experience may be in Kingdom Living (which is another term for pleasing God), faith is the catalyst that makes it all possible. The importance of faith cannot be stressed too much since it remains the key to successful Christian living. As you continue to discover, believe and practice truth, your faith will grow as your life adjusts accordingly.

Another motivation in our quest to please God is, ***"For whatever does not originate and proceed from faith is sin" (Romans 14:23 Amplified New Testament).*** Perhaps it's hard to accept that, in going anywhere, doing and saying anything, all of which does not have a faith-foundation is sin. This is a truth that sets your feet firmly on the discovery trail for faith-filled living. As each day dawns, constantly ask and expect the Holy Spirit to guide you into a faith-foundation for your words, ways and works. He is there to help you in your quest.

You must understand that faith is not just human effort alone although human activity may be involved. Neither is faith a 'leap in the dark', some blind action. Faith is simply a step into more light (truth understood and applied). The measure of faith you now possess enables you to receive more Spirit-given knowledge, more truth. As you in faith implement truth the result will be increased faith. The Holy Spirit's comment on the Israelites in the wilderness is that they did not mix God's Word with faith and so perished (17).

Faith brought you into God's family with the charge ***"the just shall live by faith" (Hebrews 10:38 Amplified New Testament)*** and only faith will sustain you. Faith and faith alone sustains 'just' people. The Bible explains 'just people' as those who have been declared righteous by God through their faith in Jesus Christ. They are also declared to be saints. When you discover in the Scriptures the word saint it is speaking of a righteous person, a just person. It is unfortunate that the word 'saint' has been given an incorrect connotation by religionists. They have made it to only mean a special recognition and elevation of the names of certain dead people whom they consider to have been exceptionally holy. In the Bible, the word 'saint' is used to denote someone set-apart for God's service. When you became a believer, you became a righteous person, a just person, a saint. You were set apart by God to serve Him in daily living. There are many Scriptures that affirm this. Because you are now a saint, a just person, a righteous person, your new status doesn't mean that you cannot sin but when you do, you don't revert to being a sinner and find yourself back at square one, in Satan's camp. Neither does it mean you can no longer 'live by faith'. When God received, forgave and accepted you He took you out of the dominion of darkness, of slavery to sin, and placed you in the kingdom of His dear Son (18). You are now light in the Lord, you are free from the law of sin and death, you are in God's care (19). Should you sin, you are still a saint, a righteous person, a just person who has sinned and immediately God's mercy comes to the fore (20). Faith accepts that God's grace has made provision for this.

To comfort and encourage us, God's word declares that ***"if we walk in the light, as He is in the light, we have fellowship with one another, and the blood of Jesus, His Son, purifies us from all sin. If we claim to be without sin, we deceive ourselves and the truth is not in us. If we confess our sins, He is faithful and just and will forgive us our sins and purify us from all unrighteousness" (1 John 1:7-9 New International Version Bible).***

Ignorance of God Himself and His ways is an enemy of faith. Whenever you act in a matter without knowing what God says about it, faith is absent and ignorance takes over. Only a Godly understanding will banish ignorance. This makes faith-growth an essential for you.

The fact of your sinning, most of it through ignorance, doesn't alter your status as a just or righteous person because God's love has secured the remedy. Christ's non-stop intercession to the Father on your behalf takes care of failures. Of course, wilful wrong-doing impairs your relationship with the Lord but repentance brings restoration. Christ's constant intercession for you is made on the basis of His sacrificial death whereby His precious blood was permanently established in heaven (21), the blood that constantly cleanses you from all sin and maintains your bond with God the Father. This on-going process is just wonderful and remains a vital part of God's great Grace-plan. However, His goodness in this matter is not a licence to sin but an incentive to be holy as He is holy.

Ignorance of how to live Godly in Christ Jesus needs to be exchanged for experiential knowledge that puts you in control no matter what circumstances arise. The outcome of your faith negotiating situations in life is always an increase in knowing God. His generosity secures it all, mercy flowing out of His love initiated faith in your heart to secure a new-birth experience in Jesus (22) expecting afterwards that by reason of use your faith will grow and grow and grow (23).

Faith-growth in you is the great essential; not faith talked about or agreed as necessary; not something just resident in the mind or accepted as an ideal; but faith as a work, an operational experience that transfers revelation into reality. First, a truth revealed, then that truth believed resulting in a changed outlook and finally action, as truth is applied. The faith I am talking about produces something. ***"..faith without works is dead ...." ( James 2:26 New King James Bible).***

The late Smith Wigglesworth, a faith-giant of the early British Pentecostal Movement, often remarked that 'Faith is an Act'. This excellent description remains true for us all. Faith being something believed, a choice based on a Spirit-revealed truth resulting in an action when the senses (the facts) say otherwise. This is not mind over matter but truth over fact, the very opposite of living by sight.

The act of 'living by faith' means for you just this. First; a refusal to respond to your emotions and the evidence of your senses (the facts) when these are found to be in opposition to a Spirit-revealed truth. Second, the application of whatever truth the Holy Spirit has revealed. Faith is a deliberate act of your will. Your response to a truth revealed, believed, obeyed, and then trusting God for the promised outcome even when delay occurs(24).

* There is a Biblical prosperity to be enjoyed by each child of God including you. His motivation for blessing is that you might bless others with the same blessing that you've received(25). Blessings never come alone, they bring with them responsibilities.

* Biblical prosperity can be yours, as you in faith fulfil any conditions that are attached to any truth discovered in God's word. You will find the outcome affects every area of your life.

* Knowing God, going wherever and doing whatever under His direction is your priority pursuit. The obedience of faith leads away from all presumption.

* Christ's continual intercession for you before His Father's throne releases you into holiness of life.

Bible References

---

15. Jeremiah 31:33 and 40, 2 Corinthians 3:3, Hebrews 10:16-18 New King James Bible.
16. Revelation 3:1-6 The Message, page 613.
17. Hebrews 4: 1-2 New King James Bible.
18. Colossians 1:13 Amplified New Testament.
19. Romans 8:1-2 Amplified New Testament.

20.1 John 2: 1-2 Amplified New Testament.
21.Hebrews 9: 11-14 Amplified New Testament.
22.Romans 12:3 New King James Bible.
23.2 Thessalonians 1:3 Amplified New Testament.
24.Hebrews 10:36. New International Version Bible
25.2 Corinthians 1: 3-4 New King James Bible.

# CHAPTER THREE

## WATER-WALKING

The prelude to faith is when we accept and act upon the words of the Holy Spirit as guidance rather than believe the conflicting evidence of our senses(26). Let me illustrate this from an incident during our years in Africa.

Zimbabwe gained a world-accepted Independence during early 1980. Robert Mugabe became Prime Minister, later elected President. Immediate years before this event were littered with all sorts of atrocities. As Independence Day approached the white Christian community had been primed with many so-called prophetic, gory predictions that the new Government would be totalitarian, anti-Christian and to expect the worst.

A few weeks after Independence celebrations took place, an evangelism team, of which I was leader, commenced aerial dropping of Gospel leaflets over the rural areas of Zimbabwe, largely closed because of war. Operation Snowstorm, as we called it, was initiated by a local church leader giving us enough money to print and drop from the skies one million leaflets.

Before commencing operations, permission was needed from the Police and various Provincial Commissioners. We found the old Administration still in place, with transfer of power pending. By telephone contact over five days God opened hearts in officialdom to endorse our aerial activity, each Officer giving their consent. This was nothing short of a miracle.

Just after commencing our aerial mission and being fully persuaded that it was of God, we then exercised faith and ordered another three million leaflets. God miraculously providing us with aircraft, pilots, leaflet-droppers and finances. About two months into 'Operation Snowstorm' we had an unexpected visitor, a man who said he was acting under orders from a senior Minister of the new Government. Our aerial drop of leaflets had evidently upset some folk and who had angrily complained to the Minister. He had ordered an immediate investigation as to what and why our aerial action.

Before introducing himself our visitor warned me that I could be thrown out of Zimbabwe within twenty-four hours. His manner and tone of voice while courteous was not friendly. God graciously enveloped me in His peace. He then produced one of our leaflets and asked tersely if I knew anything about them. The leaflet we were using carried a political slogan, 'Forward to Final Victory'. The new, ruling government party had used that slogan to bring them to power. On our leaflet was a picture of God on His throne receiving people on that Great and Final Day together with appropriate Gospel words.

After I had explained our purpose the visitor advised an immediate cessation of all aerial activities and intimated that if we continued, dire consequences could ensue. We queried this by declaring that our actions had official approval. He then demanded an explanation of this in detail. After listening to all we had to say and preparing to leave, he said his report would be on the Minister's desk by the following morning. His final word of advice was that if I wanted to avoid trouble I should cancel all aerial operations immediately.

When he had gone my mind was working overtime as I said to the Lord, "You were aware of that man's visit and words. What should we do? Should we stop our leaflet blizzard as he advised or ignore all the possible repercussions and carry on?" As I sat down with my Bible in hand it fell open and amazed I began to read ***"For the Lord God helps me; therefore have I not been ashamed or confounded; therefore have I set my face like a flint, and I know I shall not be put to shame. He***

***is near me Who declares me in the right; who will contend with me? Let us stand forth together. Who is my adversary? Let him come near to me. Behold the Lord God will help; who is he who will condemn me?" (Isaiah 50:7-9 Amplified Bible).***

As I read and re-read these verses, it was as though God was speaking in an audible voice. However, these words ushered in not only a tremendous challenge but also an inward battle. My spirit man was for 'carrying on' while my senses clamoured for an immediate cessation of aerial activities. Carrying on could mean an immediate cancellation of our residency with knock-on results affecting both our future and that of the whole Leaflet ministry and team.

So there it was in stark reality—-react to the threats and cancel the airdrop or continue in obedience to God's Word. Fear or faith. Obey man or God. After collective prayer we finally opted for faith's pathway, carried on with our aerial literature-blitz and completed it several months later with no repercussions.

The new Zimbabwe Government settled into power and contrary to predictions endorsed the Christian message. To their credit they adopted from the outset a policy of reconciliation still operative today.

Because of this the Christian message has flourished in that land with amazing results.

You may recall the Bible narrative of Peter getting out of a boat in a storm and walking on the water to Jesus at His invitation (27). In the true life drama just described, we walked on water, we took God at His word. Whenever you set aside your senses to apply truth into a situation, you move into the faith-realm. Walking according to God's Word is always a sure thing. Your trust in Him will never end in disaster.

When Peter walked on stormy Lake Galilee he moved into the supernatural. With water under his feet he recognised as never before the divinity of Jesus (28). The same revelation will be yours as you walk with Him. Whether your experience is stormy or calm, you will enjoy peace and safety.

*** Why does Faith please God? Faith pleases God because it produces maturity. Earthly parents desire their children to grow up, even more so does our heavenly Father- God want His children to grow into maturity.**

*** Our goal in life must be to 'live by faith'. This is how we express our gratitude to God.**

*** The source of faith is our Lord Jesus (29), while the supply line is the Word of God (30). Could anything be easier?**

*** The boat of human endeavour without God, our self-life, has to be abandoned if we are going to be water-walkers. The supernatural can be experienced as often as we want. Faith is the gift with a lift.**

## Bible References

26. Mark 8:34-38 New King James Bible.
27. Matthew 14:22-33 New King James Bible.
28. Matthew 16: 15-17 New King James Bible.
29. Hebrews 12:2 New King James Bible.
30. Romans 10:17 New King James Bible.

# CHAPTER FOUR

## FOOLISH QUESTIONS

When we believe and apply God's Word and it doesn't seem to work for us, what do we do? Similarly, when we pray and have great expectations as to answers and there is no answer, how do we react? When such situations of apparent failure arise we are at our most vulnerable. It is all too possible for failures to give rise to doubts because confidence in God is under attack. At such times it is your enemy, the devil, the father of lies, taking advantage of the situation to besiege your mind with taunting negative suggestions (31). Amidst fazed thoughts it is easy for attitudes to emerge which fault God, such attitudes allow unbelief to gain entry. Strange as it may seem, belief and unbelief can be resident in us, an echo of a father's cry, ***"Lord, I believe, help my unbelief" (Mark 9:24 New King James Bible).***

Attitudes arising from word/prayer failures can so easily become mind-sets. Each are there because without realising it, God's Word has been measured by human experience and given a fail mark. Whereas faith, flowing in humility, measures human experience by God's Word and finds the human side wanting. ***"Let God be true and every man a liar" (Romans 3:4 New King James Bible).***

When the heart accepts the lie that God is at fault a mind-set takes over. Mind-sets (or strongholds as the Bible calls them) are stumbling blocks to faith. I call them "reservation-modes" because you have now added to what was believed preceding any failure, a reservation that somehow it will not work for you. That immediately places a limit on that truth again being personally applied. Each time that truth surfaces an 'OK for others but not for me' attitude is present. Avoid such mind-sets like poison because their conclusions will always surface and control your mind when subjects relating to failures are in focus. Always keep an open mind despite failures.

Mind-sets can also come by way of familiarity with certain Bible texts, stories, etc.; an 'I know what it says' attitude which will hinder further revelation. Faith grows by revelation. All Scripture is a progressive revelation which means there is always more truth to discover, no matter how familiar you are with the Scriptures. For example 'the parable of the Sower ' is one of the most known stories of the Gospels.(32) If the question was asked, 'How many types of ground are indicated'? Your probable answer would be four. Then applying the word personally you would probably say, 'I am good ground'. Both answers being correct.

However, further thought could also come up with two as a valid answer. This answer would give good and bad ground and then personally applied our choice again would be good ground. Yet even more thought and we have another correct answer, six types of ground; Pathway, Stoney, Weed-filled, 30%, 60%, 100%. This answer personally applied opens up a completely new ball-game because we can possibly identify all six types of ground that at some time occupy our hearts.

Let's consider each of them beginning with the 'pathway'. We hear much of God's Word but not all registers—'pathway'. Sometimes we get enthusiastic about things but they die on us—'stoney ground'. The very presence of stress indicates 'weedy-ground' and then where are we in the percentage stakes? One thing is certain no business man is going to settle for low percentage yield, neither will God. He will concentrate on softening our hearts, eliminate the stones, destroy the weeds, and by His gentle, constant intervention produces fruit, more fruit, much fruit.(33). Never allow an **'I know it'** or a **'Not for me**' or a **'Yes but'** stronghold to trap you.

Now I want to ask you some foolish questions. On occasions Jesus asked what appeared to be a foolish question. For instance, He went to a man whom sickness had ravaged for thirty-eight years and who desperately wanted his health restored and said to him ***"Do you want to be made well?" (John 5:6 New King James Bible)***. In the light of the years of his sickness such a question seems ridiculous and irrelevant. Then why did Jesus ask it? The reason is reflected in the man's answer, "Sir, I want to be healed but I'm helpless". His confession of impotence became his cry for help. Jesus reacted to his confession of dependency by saying, ***"Get up and walk!"***. This very sick man obeyed because he believed, faith moved him to get up and as he did so his health was restored(34). This Bible incident was written to help us in our faith-walk.

Here then are my foolish questions,

**DO YOU WANT TO LIVE A CAREFREE LIFE ?**

**DO YOU BELIEVE YOU CAN LIVE A CAREFREE LIFE ?**

Consider well before you answer and review all that has been shared before. May I suggest you take your stand with the paralytic and say, **"yes! but I can't on my own, I need help"**. On the other hand if you cannot answer immediately, review your life historically. I feel sure you will conclude that to live now and in the future without a single care is impossible. Talk the whole matter over with God and don't be afraid to verbalise your weakness, your utter inability to achieve a carefree life without His help. God awaits your confession of impotence, a faith declaration in humility and dependency. As you declare your helplessness, listen carefully for God's gentle command ***"GIVE ME THE WHOLE OF YOUR CARE FOR I CARE FOR YOU" (1 Peter 5:7 paraphrased)***

In order to understand more fully this gracious invitation from the Lord we need to contrast the words **'care'** and **'care'**. The first 'care' compounds fear, anxiety, insecurity, stress, anything that disturbs peace of mind. God is never the source of any of these but so willing to lift them from us because He 'cares'. Here the word used carries the meaning of being intensely interested, having a heart for, affectionate concern. As His child you are the object of God's responsibility. Could a loving, caring God be any more direct than this? He is willing to take the sum total of all things that cause stress if you will but give them to Him and in exchange receive His peace. The first step in giving God the whole of your care is by believing that you can and move your mind into the concept of carefree living, belief arising from His quite amazing invitation.

God doesn't ask of you the impossible, therein lies the incentive to deliberately set aside the evidence of your senses and move to higher ground confessing **"I will live God's way—-NO CARES!"** Learning how to leave your cares with Him is dealt with later after more vital ground-coverage. Here and now ask God's help. Make up your mind on the strength of His command with promise and loudly say " I WILL". Congratulations! You've taken a great leap forward as you've declared your faith-stance from this moment forward.

However, having done that, all your worries, fears and all that causes stress in your life will not immediately and automatically disappear. So be on your guard, don't allow unbelief to say, "nothing has changed". This is where the patience of faith comes to the fore and claims victory as you learn how to give your cares to God. Faith trusts Him and doesn't waver regardless of obstacles to the goal.

To safeguard progress along God's planned pathway, it is imperative to fully comprehend the words of Jesus when He said ***"Man shall not live by bread alone but by every word of God" ( Luke 4:4 New King James Bible)***. Be prepared for this verse to click your mind into one of those reservation-modes we've talked about earlier, probably an 'I know that', especially as it's a well known and familiar verse.

An open and enquiring mind is an essential whenever these words are considered. God is speaking and He never speaks idle words. Here He is giving vital, practical advice on all-round nourishment, both natural and spiritual food being necessary. Implicit in this verse quoted is the open secret of how to secure a continual faith-growth, the very basis for carefree living. Now eliminate any mind-set and embrace this truth with no reservations.

There must be no doubt in your mind that **God's Word is your lifeline in faith living——faith-food,** glorious faith-food. The immediate outcome will be a changed attitude to daily Bible reading. Eventually you will love God's Word as you make it priority reading. Believe Him when He counsels ***"Faith comes by hearing, and hearing by the word of God" (Romans 10:17 New King James Bible).***

Avoid being caught up in the syndrome of Bible reading as a duty to perform for its own sake rather than a discovery trail. Duty-reading is generally done under a time restraint with what is to follow it uppermost in the mind. Duty-reading does not readily lend itself to discover truth because the mind is part occupied with post-reading activity.

Without a genuine faith-approach to Bible-reading, little will be gained apart from academic knowledge which is no substitute for Holy Spirit revelation. Those who believe that life is far too crowded to devote any quality time to reading and meditation totally miss out on their faith-potential. We give neither reverence or service to God when reading the Bible if faith is absent. The whole approach to this high priority activity (it includes listening) must be of faith for the reader/listener to gain spiritual benefit. Faith expects the Holy Spirit to say something because faith is aware that God responds to those who diligently seek Him.

Martin Luther, the great Reformation leader, said, 'The Bible is alive, it speaks to me; it has feet, it runs after me; it has hands, it lays hold on me'. Thomas Watson, Puritan minister and writer said, '...the Bible let it not only inform you, but inflame you'. Woodrow Wilson, US President 1913-21 said, I am sorry for the men who do not read the Bible every day. I wonder why they deprive themselves of the strength and of the pleasure. It is one of the most singular books in the world, for every time you open it, some old text that you have read a score of times suddenly beams with new meaning. There is no book that I know of, of which this is true: there is no other book that yields its meaning so personally, that seems to fit so intimately to the very spirit that is seeking its guidance'(D). The Lord Jesus said, ***"It is the Spirit who gives life; the flesh profits nothing. The words that I speak to you are spirit, and they are life" (John 6:63 New King James Bible).***

Smith Wigglesworth made this comment concerning the Bible. "Never compare this book with other books. Comparisons are dangerous. Other books are of the earth; this is of heaven. Never say this book contains the Word of God. It is the Word of God. Eternal in its duration; incomprehensible in power; infinite in its scope; human in penmanship; present in application. Read it through; write it down. Pray it in! Work it out! Pass it on!" (E).

All God's children are instructed to renew their minds(35). The thought patterns and structures that shaped our former lives need to be exchanged for a spiritual mind. This is essential if we are to grow up into Christ in all things. How and when does this take place? Each time the Holy Spirit reveals to you more truth you have a choice. If you allow faith to accept and apply this fresh truth a measure of mind-change or renewal will take place. This becomes a repeat process with both faith and mind-renewal ever increasing. God's Word and faith are inseparable to the ongoing transformation of your mind. The pace of change always being up to you.

Scripture says ***"..we have the mind of Christ" ( 1 Corinthians 2:16 Amplified New Testament)***. Access began when Christ entered your life. Increased possession is a progressive experience at the expense of your former thought processes. As this takes place so your spiritual hearing becomes more and more sensitive to hear God's voice. Truth revealed and believed brings about changes. It begins with a changed outlook by seeing things in a different light. Then your attitude changes and without conscious effort your social behaviour adjusts to the truth believed. The end result of faith-reading and/or faith-hearing the Scriptures is always change into Christ-likeness. It is of paramount importance to believe that God's Word is divine food for your inner man. As you feed your inner man, so your life in Jesus will improve in quality as possessors of His mind.

The 'Will' of the Lord Jesus was ratified by His death. He now lives to bestow all the benefits of His sacrificial death to those who believe. May I suggest you confine your Bible reading to that 'Will' called 'The New Testament'. You need to be thoroughly acquainted with all that is yours by divine bequest, a fabulously rich inheritance. It is true that the 'all things', the treasures, to be discovered in the New Testament are also to be found in the Old Testament but it is often difficult to find them because they are hidden, when in the New God's great Salvation-plan is open reading.

As you begin to familiarise yourself with the New Testament add to your reading three Books from the Old; namely Genesis; the book of beginnings, Psalms; the great prayer/praise portfolio and Proverbs; practical guidance into holy living. Later on when you've made a lot of progress in your daily, intimate walk with God, more excursions can be made into the Old Testament. You will then find that with your experiential knowledge of the New, how much easier it is to understand the Old. "The New is in the Old concealed, the Old is in the New revealed", whoever said that had great insight.

The Bible is likened to a banqueting table. A table well laden with super food-delights and extravagant delicacies, all being the provision of divine love. God chooses to reveal Himself to hungry hearts who regularly feed from His word, His banqueting table. Smith Wigglesworth said "How shall we dare sleep when the Spirit commands us to take everything on the table. It is the greatest banquet that ever was and will be—-the table where all you take only leaves more behind"(F).

When feasting at God's banqueting table express your gratitude by thanking Him for such marvellous food. Always remember, present to serve you is the Holy Spirit who longs to give you nourishing portions of truth.

As He reveals these, believe and immediately apply them to yourself. Truth assimilated produces faith-growth recognised by others through your changed lifestyle. Understand that faith-growth is not a series of dramatic 'highs', these may come occasionally but faith-growth generally comes by a steady, gentle, almost unobtrusive changing of your mind in favour of truth revealed and comprehended.

*** Daily guidance by the Holy Spirit maintains and develops relationship with Jesus and ensures we live, know and go in Him(36).**

*** Salvation is a complete gift from Father, Son and Holy Spirit. Only total dependence on our giving-God brings full enjoyment.**

*** Eating regularly at God's table (His Word) must be priority. As in the natural so in the spiritual, starvation brings problems. Avoid being a spiritual anorexic.**

* The importance of knowing the content of the Will of Jesus—the New Testament—cannot be minimised. Human reaction to any bequest is a desire to know the extent and value of any gift. We deny God, ourselves and others by remaining ignorant of the terms of His gift to us in Christ. He wants us to be fully aware and enjoy all the rich treasure He has bequeathed us.

## Bible References

31. John 8:44 New King James Bible.
32. Mark 4:1-20 New King James Bible.
33. John 15: 1-5 New King James Bible.
34. John 5: 5-9 New King James Bible.
35. Romans 12:2 and Ephesians 4:23 Amplified New Testament.
36. John 14:6 New International Version Bible.

# CHAPTER FIVE

# THE FEEL- GOOD FACTOR

There is a feel-good factor available to you that is real and lasting but it is in total contrast with human emotions that go up and down like a yo-yo, giving birth to feelings, either good or bad, depending on prevailing circumstances whether good or bad. The feel-good factor is a faith possession and easily converts to your spiritual identity. The feel-good factor is established by your understanding of who you are in God and an increasing comprehension of His beneficial purposes towards you. Those beneficial purposes include knowing and possessing your amazing inheritance in Christ. Amazing because of the scope and quality of its content and its inherent power to transform. As you continue to go from faith to faith so your spiritual identity will become progressively established.

The feel-good factor is initiated and sustained by choice, a faith choice, you choosing to ***"see and believe Him who is invisible" (37)*** whatever the event. By allowing your spiritual heritage to outweigh those things that characterise your circumstances, you become more and more aware of God. The effect is a transformed outlook because you know;

1. You are in Christ — you are a son of God — you are a king invested with authority — you are a victor not a victim.

2. You have an inheritance in Christ — you possess multiple gifts and graces to use or display at times like these.

3. Your life in Christ is for your present situation with no exceptions. By always reaching into God's wisdom you really live. Your daily round should be no dull affair but rather a constant celebration. Nothing should threaten you; you have nothing to prove; you walk tall with the Spirit in control of your life; a daily adventure with the living God as your companion.

Unlike fluctuating human emotions this feel-good factor is like the gyrocompass on a ship, always perfectly level regardless of what the ship may be doing due to adverse weather conditions. Because of the gyrocompass' stability the Captain is able to keep his ship on course to its desired destination. The knowledge of your spiritual identity will keep your life free of turmoil in the midst of adverse circumstances, as well as keep you on course until you reach journey's end.

A good example of this is found in the adventure story of Paul and his companion, Silas. These two, early pioneers of the Christian message, were able to sing to God having suffered personal injury amidst horrifying circumstances. They were able to do this because they were well aware of their spiritual identity and nothing, no nothing, could disturb their peace and joy. Their expression of the feel-good factor brought about an earth-shattering response from God. Read it for yourself in Acts, chapter 16.

The Holy Spirit is constantly available to guide you into all truth (38), albeit one revelation at a time. He is not a reluctant Guide but One who is ready and willing to lead you from truth to truth along an unending pathway of privilege, from faith to faith as you follow His leading. The Holy Spirit is extremely patient and always gentle as He waits for you to get to grips with what He reveals.

Each positive response will take you from your present position of faith to another, each repeat exercise promotes faith-growth. Maturity of faith consolidates the feel-good factor which rests on the foundation of your being special to God. Just consider this; before God ever created this world of ours His foreknowledge enabled Him to see you, to observe you through and through and fully acquainted with your sin over the years with its ghastly consequences (39). He knew precisely the extent of your rebellion toward Him and the ugliness of your depraved soul, warts and all. When that appraisal was fully complete, He lovingly, carefully, and mercifully selected you because He also saw what you could become in His Son Jesus. In love He chose you to be His own child thus making you part of His family. ***"You are all sons of God through faith in Jesus Christ". "How great is the love the Father has lavished on us, that we should be called children of God! And this is what we are! (Galatians 3:26 and 1 John 3:1 New International Version Bible)***

You are very special to God by reason of choice. Choice speaks of purpose and God had one when He chose you. Part of His purpose in choosing you is that each day you would live on a level where you reign in life (40). Reigning is the lifestyle of kings. You then have been chosen to be a king and to live accordingly ***"To Him who loved us and washed us from our sins in His own blood, and has made us kings and priests to His God and Father, to Him be glory and dominion forever and ever" (Revelation 1:6 New King James Bible).***

When God brought you into His family, He ordained that royal status should be yours together with everything necessary to live a kingly life here and now. The feel-good factor rests on the solid foundation of divine preference—-God chose you, divine provision—-God cares for you, and divine purpose—-God is changing you.

However, it must be realised that we do have an enemy. He is described as a thief and a robber whose purpose is to deprive us of our inheritance by deception (41). He deceives us by using adverse feelings to accuse God of deserting us and not caring about our situation. Quite often, because adverse feelings are more dominant than God's Word we allow ourselves to be deceived. When adverse feelings are uppermost it is beneficial to comfort yourself in God. How do you do this?

The answer lies in declaring those words which you know to be true concerning God's choice of you as His child and therefore you being very special to Him. This is made easier if you memorise those Scriptures that assure you of His presence and those that establish your status in Christ. Thus armed and protected by truth you can allay anything your feelings might produce. The armour that is available to you (outlined in Ephesians, chapter six), and our weaponry is all truth based. By our open and joyful acknowledgement of truth (our confession), we are enabled to stand and withstand against the enemy. Whatever your circumstances you can choose by faith to reign, the logical outcome of the feel-good factor. Faith makes a choice based on the following scripture that should long ago be resident in our hearts.

***"Even as in His love He chose us—actually picked us out for Himself as His own—in Christ before the foundation of the world; that we should be holy and blameless in His sight, even above reproach, before Him in love"***
***( Ephesians 1:4-6 Amplified New Testament).***

***"But God! So rich is He in His mercy! Because of and in order to satisfy the great and wonderful and intense love with which He loved us, even when we were dead by our own shortcomings and trespasses, He made us alive together in fellowship and union with Christ. He gave us the very life of Christ Himself, the same new life with which He quickened Him. (It is by grace you are saved) and He raised us up together with Him and made us sit down together in the heavenly sphere in Christ Jesus, the Anointed One"(Ephesians 2: 4-6 Amplified New Testament).***

To reinforce these staggering truths our Lord Jesus declares we also have been chosen to produce fruit. Fruit that doesn't rot but is constantly maturing and increasing. God again discloses our speciality in His choice, the end result being everlasting fruit (42). It is comforting to know that the ever Living One never gives up on us. He never passes by an opportunity to prune us, to perfect us in Himself. His plans include an ongoing increase of the fruit of the Gospel (evangelism) and the fruit of Righteousness (holiness) in our lives.

***"But now having been set free from sin and having becomes slaves of God, you have your fruit unto holiness, and the end, everlasting life" (Romans 6:22 New King James Bible). "That you may be sincere and without offence till the day of Christ, being filled with the fruits of Righteousness which are by Jesus Christ to the glory and praise of God" (Philippians 1: 10 - 11 New King James Bible).***

Several years ago we came back to Britain for a short stay. The high-light of all our visits was to see our children and grandchildren. This particular visit was no exception. Upon meeting one of our granddaughters we found her wearing a tee-shirt we had given her on a previous visit and on the front of the shirt were words which said, 'God loves me so much He cannot take His eyes off me'. Of course there were some oohs and aahs because she is a pretty girl (I hope I don't sound too biased), but those words on her tee-shirt actually echo a profound spiritual truth. Truth that applies to all who love God through faith in Jesus, His Son. Yes! God loves you so much He cannot take His eyes off you.

God's great primary purpose in choosing you, upon which rests all previous declared plans, is His intention of making you Christ-like. ***"God knew what He was doing from the very beginning. He decided from the outset to shape the lives of those who love Him along the same lines as the life of His Son. The Son stands first in the line of humanity He restored. We see the original and intended shape of our lives there in Him. After God made that decision of what His children should be like, He followed it up by calling people by name. After He called them by name He set them on a solid basis with Himself. And then, after getting them established, He stayed with them to the end, gloriously completing what He had begun"***
***(Romans 8:29 The Message, page 379).***

What an amazing privilege you enjoy. What singular and personal attention is yours. You are not forgotten, put on one side, left to your own devices. You are always and at all times the focus of God's loving attention which is nothing less than absolutely marvellous!

The feel-good factor being a faith-stance arises out of believing and confessing the truth about God and your relationship with Him. Initially you need to often speak this out, mostly to yourself, until assurance becomes permanent. When we hear ourselves speaking truth, assurance is stimulated and our hearts comforted. When that happens all doubt is removed from your mind of God's good intentions toward you regardless of events. Such a stance will incite opposition but nothing to be afraid of. Most opposition will come through your feelings and these arise generally by reason of your circumstances.

As factual as feelings are they can prompt you to consider things that are often contrary to what God has declared. When this happens you must believe Him and refute any suggestion of the enemy that he would inject into your mind such as: God doesn't love you!: You've been deserted by God!; You can't be saved because you don't feel it!: Where is your God? and so on.

When such opposition arises, verbalise your spiritual identity remembering that God hasn't changed one little bit. His promises to you remain sure. Open your mouth and confess those words that declare God's choice of you, His love and acceptance of you, promises He has given you. By this you will comfort, assure and encourage yourself with truth which will deal a death blow to the thief. You can believe your feelings and under their control miss out on God or you can believe Him and advance into LIFE. Let me illustrate this from a personal experience.

I flew from Britain to Africa during June '73. This was in response to a 'call' of God, also to my wife, to relocate to Zimbabwe (at that time called, Rhodesia), get myself a job and in our free time engage in soul-winning. In obedience to this 'call', I had resigned my engineering management position and our house had been sold. Now I was en-route to Africa leaving my wife and three daughters in temporary accommodation pending the older two going back into Teacher's Training College. Afterwards, my wife and youngest daughter would join me in Zimbabwe.

As my flight became airborne, the cabin crew became active and my fellow-passengers began to relax. However, as I tried to relax a sense of utter desolation descended on me like a cloud. Suddenly my emotions were at rock bottom with my mind under tremendous attack. At the same time it was as though darkness enveloped me and blotted out all consciousness of the aircraft.

My mind was in a turmoil as varying thoughts began to torment me. Thoughts such as; my recent actions had ruined my life, all I had worked for was in ruins; what a fool I was for throwing my career away at forty-nine years of age; in selling our house we would never be able to buy another; through my actions I was being irresponsible towards my wife and our children. On the verge of tears I called a halt to these lies and began to verbalise to myself the call of God.

I confessed His Word and promises given to us that had prompted our every action. I recalled the miracles of God's gracious provision between my resigning my job and the selling of our house, when mortgages were almost non-existent. I recalled how God, in answer to prayer, brought a buyer from across the world to make a cash purchase. I mentally tabulated every miraculous act of kindness we had received from His hand. Yes! I confessed the unchangeableness of God and His faithfulness over the many years of our lives. As I continued to verbalise truth, so my mind and spirit entered into rest, truth had banished every adverse thought and feeling.

I began to sing as the darkness lifted and the joy of heaven flooded my soul. The enemy had been defeated and God was once more in control. A stewardess interrupted my singing (silent to human ears) to offer me refreshment, little did she know just how refreshed I was. Subsequently, God prospered our years in Africa in many other miraculous ways but that is another story.

*** The Holy Spirit will help you to progressively understand and possess your legacy under the Will of Jesus. Hence the need to love, honour and obey Him.**

*** The facts (evidences derived from your senses) in Life's experiences are often in opposition to truth revealed. As facts are rejected in favour of truth so the Way of Holiness opens up before us.**

*** You are God's chosen, beloved child. Adverse situations do not alter that truth. At all times our response should be praise to our God with thanksgiving.**

*** Our becoming Christ-like is not by any self-effort, it is wholly a work carried out by the Holy Spirit as we continue a faith-walk. God has pledged Himself to complete the job and perfect us in Jesus (44).**

## Bible References

37. Hebrews 11:24-27 New King James Bible
38. John 16:12-14 New King James Bible
39. Romans 6:23 and Revelation 20:11-15 Amplified New Testament
40. Romans 5:17 New International Version Bible
41. John 10:10 Amplified New Testament
42. John 15:16 and Galatians 5:22-23 New King James Bible
43. Ephesians 1:3-11 Amplified New Testament
44. Philippians 1:6 Amplified New Testament

# CHAPTER SIX

## NOTHING MISSING

***"Therefore having been justified by faith, we have peace with God through our Lord Jesus Christ, through Whom also we have ACCESS BY FAITH INTO THIS GRACE WHEREIN WE STAND, and rejoice in hope of the glory of God" (Romans 5: 1-2 New King James Bible).***

When we first believed we tasted of the Grace of God. Anything and everything made available to us, to you, because you are 'in Christ' is all because of and wrapped up in God's Grace. Grace has been described as abounding undeserved favour, something given being totally unmerited, an overflowing benevolence bestowed upon unworthy beings. ***"For God so loved the world that He gave His only begotten Son, that whoever believes in Him should not perish but have everlasting life. For God did not send His Son into the world to condemn the world, but that the world through Him might be saved" (John 3:16-17 New King James Bible).*** This is Grace in action and there is more. ***"His divine power has given us everything we need for life and godliness through our knowledge of Him who called us by His own glory and goodness" (2 Peter 1:3 New International Version Bible).***

With these powerful statements God affirms that we lack nothing in order for us to live a holy life. He then goes on to reveal the means by which it is accomplished when He says, ***"Through these (His glory and goodness) He has given us very great and precious promises, so that through them you may participate in the divine nature and escape the corruption in the world caused by evil desires" (2 Peter 1:4 New International Version Bible).***

This astounding ability of being able to assimilate and retain the substance of God's nature itself, is residual in His Grace. Without trying to comprehend this wonder, just outwork the urge within you to search the Scriptures to discover, believe and make your personal possession every God-promise given you 'in Christ'. It all comes down to a 'search and secure' operation while reading the 'Will' of Jesus. When you find a promise look for the conditions and through the obedience of faith satisfy them. In doing this you not only gain the promise but a little more of God's nature. So, within easy reach is a means for you ***"to grow in grace and recognition and understanding of our Lord and Saviour Jesus Christ" (2 Peter 3:18 Amplified New Testament).***

Little wonder God's promises are called exceedingly great and very precious for when acted upon bring about amazing results (45).

Early in his Gospel John succinctly declares that, ***"grace and truth came by Jesus Christ"***. He brought into our humanity a new awareness of the greatness of God and the super-abundance of gifts that flow from His heart toward us. Each and everyone of these gifts is the response of grace. We can see grace incredibly woven into the whole fabric of life. Pause for a moment and consider the vast universe of which our world is but a minute part. The reaches of space may awe us but its sheer magnitude speaks not only of the greatness of God but also the greatness of His grace. Now turn your attention to the profusion of colour around you or look up into a cloudless night-sky where myriad gems parade their glittering beauty upon a backcloth of deep velvet. These all add testimony to the multi-faceted wonder of grace.

Perhaps the greatest of these many illustrations of grace and so indicative of the whole in its outworking is the ' law of reproduction '. Whatever seed is sown a return of the same kind will be the result. However, that is far from being the whole story. Just compare the size of the single seed planted to that which grows from it, by comparison the outcome is super-size, titanic. Now view the result numerically in terms of reproduction potential, the word we would use is super-abundance. From wherever the grace of God is viewed or better still experienced, the end result will always be the same, great, glorious and brim-full of potential.

Again, we see grace on display in the parable of 'the prodigal son' (46). The renegade son having gone into a far country, wasted all his inheritance and now destitute, decides to return home and ask to be employed as a servant. As the road brings his old home into view, his father, constantly on the look-out for his erring son, sees and runs to receive him and fully restores him to the family.

In both these illustrations of grace we see that a small human action done towards God brings about a giant divine response. Such is the overwhelming grace of God. John Newton, whose radical conversion to Christ from a life of debauchery, wrote of it as 'Amazing Grace'.

Grace gives constant opportunity to live by faith within heaven's bounty which is to maximise on life. There is absolutely no substitute way for us to go. ***"If you decide for God, living a life of God-worship, it follows that you don't fuss about what's on the table at mealtimes or whether the clothes in your closet are in fashion. There is far*** *more to your life than the food you put in your stomach, more to your outer appearance than the clothes you hang on your body. Look at the birds, free and unfettered, not tied down to a job description, careless in the care of God. And you count far more to him than birds. Has anyone by fussing in front of the mirror ever gotten taller by so much as an inch? All this time and money wasted on fashion—do you think it makes that much difference? Instead of looking at the fashions, walk out into the fields and look at the wild flowers. They never primp or shop, but have you ever seen colour and design quite like it? The ten best-dressed men and women in the country look shabby alongside them.*

*If God gives such attention to the appearance of wild-flowers—most of which are never even seen—don't you think He'll attend to you, take pride in you, do His best for you? What I am trying to do here is to get you to relax, to not be so preoccupied with 'getting', so you can respond to God's giving. People who don't know God and the way He works fuss over these things, but you know both God and how He works. Steep your life in God-reality, God-initiative, God-provisions. Don't worry about missing out. You'll find all your everyday human*

***concerns will be met. Give your entire attention to what God is doing right now, and don't get worked up about what may or may not happen tomorrow. God will help you deal with whatever hard things come up when the time comes" (Matthew 6:25-34 The Message, page 26).***

God expects us to live carefree in His care because He cares. His Grace-plan places all at our disposal with absolutely nothing missing.

We are joint-heirs with Jesus and in His 'Will' it is expressed like this, ***"For you are coming progressively to recognise more strongly and clearly the GRACE of our Lord Jesus Christ—His kindness, His gracious generosity; in that though He was so very rich, yet for your sakes He became so very poor, in order that by His poverty you might become enriched—abundantly supplied" (2 Corinthians 8:9 Amplified New Testament)***

Faith is the key to access Grace (47). Use your key to enter and progressively possess its endless riches. The boundaries and possessions of Grace are limitless. The experience of Grace brings Peace. The embrace of Grace gives Joy. The sum total of Grace is God Himself. Super motivation to REALLY LIVE.

Speaking of our Lord Jesus, Paul says, ***"For the Grace of God that brings Salvation has appeared to all men. It teaches us to say NO to ungodliness and worldly passions, and to live self-controlled, upright and Godly lives in this present age, while we wait for the blessed hope—the glorious appearing of our great God and Saviour, Jesus Christ, Who gave Himself for us to redeem us from all wickedness and to purify for Himself a people that are His very own, eager to do what is good" (Titus 2: 11-13 New International Version Bible).***

It is impossible to avail yourself of anything that the God of all grace provides without change taking place in your life, no matter how small or great that change. All change is the outcome of faith-living.

The application of God's Word in your life, whether in practical action (what you do) or mental embrace (what you believe) results in Kingdom living. Such living (by faith) issues in a progressive quality of life both enjoyable and always open to increase.

*** When God gave to you His Righteousness He didn't hold anything back, He gave you Himself. Such grace means that all things given to you in Christ are now yours for the taking.**

*** The ability that is given to us to live in and by the Holy Spirit is also a grace-gift.**

*** Grace motivates participation in a seven-fold progression to full liberty " so don't lose a minute in building on what you have been given, complementing your basic faith with good character, spiritual understanding, alert discipline, passionate patience, reverent wonder, warm friendliness and generous love, each dimension fitting into and developing the others. With these qualities active and growing in your lives, no grass will grow under your feet, no day will pass without its reward as you mature in your experience of our Master Jesus. Without these qualities you can't see what's right before you, oblivious that your old sinful life has been wiped off the books"**
**(2 Peter 1: 5-9 The Message, page 584).**

**Bible References**

---

45. 2 Peter 1:2-11 New International Version Bible
46. Luke 15:11-24 New King James Bible
47. Romans 5:2 New King James Bible

# CHAPTER SEVEN

## PAUSE FOR REVIEW

Before proceeding any further, pause for a moment and assess how far you have come since opting for a carefree lifestyle. By now you should have an assurance that you can live free of things that disturb your peace of mind. Beyond and subsequent to that assurance you are committed to live stress-free, God's Word being the means of belief and gaining of all that is yours in Christ.

Without any doubt you know you are a very, special person in God's eyes, realising His love for you is no less than the love He has for His Son, the Lord Jesus (48). You now accept His amazing plan for your life that in its unfolding will change you into Christ-likeness. The very thought of this should set your spiritual adrenaline into immediate overdrive resulting in a song of gladness.

The supreme prize is the goal before you with the obedience of faith a vital necessity in getting there. Obedience is exemplified in the life of the Lord Jesus where His humanity is on open display. By simple observation the secret of His victorious life and death is discovered, namely implicit obedience to His Father's will.

Jesus was never at any time in despair; worried sick; stressed out; surprised by anything; caught off-guard by events; His circumstances on top of Him. No! never! Throughout the mockery of His trial and subsequent degrading, agonising crucifixion, He was at all times in control. He was a man under authority (His Father's) and because of this He had authority. Jesus' complete dependence on His Father in accomplishing His will put Him in a position of command (49).

Perhaps you were surprised to learn that our heavenly Father plans that we too shall follow in the steps of Jesus and learn obedience. He does not do this in any harsh and dictatorial manner but by a gentle, loving appeal which brings about a disposition within that desires to obey. You will have experienced something of this and know that obedience produces the fruit of Righteousness, the fruit of the Holy Spirit in your life.

A different approach to Bible-reading is now in action. Your new objective being to pinpoint the positives and apply them to yourself because God's Word (written with you in mind) is full of positives. Assurance is yours that you have been acquitted at God's Bar of Justice, declared 'not guilty' and given Christ's Righteousness (50). You have also been accepted into God's family (51). Belief cries out, loud enough for principalities and powers to hear

'God accepts me just as I am because I am now righteous, it's not possible for Him to reject me at any time, no!-No!-NO!'. Say it with conviction knowing that God is at your side and is within you.

Pause a little while for reflection and then continue to think of more positives: You have been anointed by the Holy Spirit (52), a continual experience as you follow your Guide. He honours you by appointing you to display His virtues through your obedience, thus producing the fruit of Righteousness in your life (53).

All these and other positives disclosed to you by the Spirit will, when acted upon, bring about constant change. Whatever the change, each began with no deliberate outward action on your part but originated within from a new disposition that came about by believing a revealed truth. Truth revealed is always God's loving wisdom towards you that will, if believed, begin to change you from within. Whatever subsequent outward action is made by you it flows from a changed outlook and attitude. If you have not yet proved this to be so, then go back to the beginning of this book and start again.

However, I'm not convinced that you could have come this far without changes for the better. I choose to believe that you are different since you first began to read, believe and apply truth as found in the Scriptures and suggested in this book. The result being that you are now inspired with a determination to attain to throne-life, you intend to reign in life by Jesus Christ (54). Three cheers for our great God and Saviour......keep going....it's better up front.

## Bible references

48. John 17:23 Amplified New Testament
49. John 10:37-38 New King James Bible
    John 5:30 Amplified New Testament
50. Romans 5:1 Amplified New Testament
51. Ephesians 1:6 New King James Bible
52. 1 John 2:20 and 24 New International Version Bible
53. 1 Peter 2:9 Amplified New Testament
54. Galatians 2:20-21 New King James Bible
    Romans 5:17 Amplified New Testament

# CHAPTER EIGHT

## SEEING THE INVISIBLE

We live in a very materialistic world. Behind and within our world are powers that seek to lead a Believer away from God's peaceful, ordained order of things. Each day, the pace of life in general mounts pressure upon us to respond to its dictates. Believers are advised not to allow these pressures to dictate our agenda and push us into the world's mould (55). We, being different, are encouraged to express that difference by character and disposition that accords with our call to live Kingdom life(56).

Those who have access to and are subject to God, seek His Kingdom, His purposes on the earth (57). Within those purposes is a special, pre-arranged plan for each of His children. That means He has one for you, to discover and walk out in your own life. How do I know that? Listen to the fount of all wisdom ***"Therefore my dear friends, as you have always obeyed—not only in my presence, but now much more in my absence— continue to work out your salvation with fear and trembling, FOR IT IS GOD WHO WORKS IN YOU TO WILL AND ACT ACCORDING TO HIS GOOD PURPOSES" (Philippians 2:12-13 New International Version Bible).***

***"For we are God's handiwork, recreated in Christ Jesus, THAT WE MAY DO THOSE GOOD WORKS WHICH GOD PLANNED BEFOREHAND FOR US, TAKING PATHS THAT HE PREPARED AHEAD OF TIME THAT WE SHOULD WALK IN THEM—LIVING THE GOOD LIFE WHICH HE PRE-ARRANGED AND MADE READY FOR US TO LIVE" (Ephesians 2:10 Amplified New Testament).***

For all who believe, there is an alternative way to that which the world incessantly and relentlessly forces upon us. Jesus said, ***"Take My yoke upon you and learn from Me...for My yoke is easy and My burden is light" (Matthew 11:29-30 New King James Bible)***. By our submission to Jesus, He shows us a way that is in total contrast to the world's demands.

Our world-system is under the power of the evil one (58) who has established its materialistic goals. With wealth-power its motivation almost every job, or the lack of one, is framed with pressure and stress. The child of God being in the world (but not of it) is also subject to the pressure to adopt its 'go and get' system. To resist it, the words of the Lord Jesus must be uppermost in a Believer's mind: ***"What will it profit a man if he gains the whole world, and loses his own soul" (Mark 8:36 New King James Bible).***

Of course these words challenge not only Christians but everyone in this highly commercial and fiercely competitive world.

Our homes that God designed to be havens of peace and rest, through lack of understanding, are often in turmoil because worldly wisdom is allowed to rule. All the latest technology exhibited by computers, fax machines, telephone answering devices, television, video, DIY, domestic products, to name a few, are meant to make life easier but the hectic pace and pressure of life remains. Time always seems to be at a premium (in spite of all the time-savers) as the world's system insidiously pushes people into the fast lane with ever increasing stress.

This is where the New Life possessor has to move in faith and resist the world's mould. Pressure begins in the mind and that is where resistance to it must begin. It is possible to be extremely busy outwardly for long periods of time but perfectly calm and composed inside. Faith will bring this about as you remember you are God's workmanship, you have recourse to His wisdom at all times which allows you to operate in God to maximum. Those outside of Jesus have no such advantage. How can you operate to maximum? The answer lies in asking God for His wisdom in whatever you're doing. Not just a daily one-off mention but asking Him again and again during your day in respect of anything that may arise. Such persistence will not meet with rejection. He will never say no, nor will He ever tell you to 'get lost' but He does say, having asked, believe that at that moment you have His wisdom (59) and act accordingly.

The God who designed, created and sustains our giant universe is well able and willing to guide us in our work and in anything else regardless of what it may be. ***"Lean on, trust and be confident in the Lord with all your heart and mind, and do not rely on your own insight or understanding. In all your ways know, recognise and acknowledge Him, and He will direct and make straight and plain your paths" (Proverbs 3:5-6 Amplified New Testament).***

It is only a person's faith that takes God at His Word, invites His wisdom at every turn and finds success. Tapping into God's wisdom is so much easier when you recognise that He is with you, the constant realisation of His presence transforms the mundane into majesty. I thoroughly proved this in Engineering Works-Management where I was always under extreme pressure to deliver manufactured component parts to delivery deadlines. Throughout each day I would constantly draw upon God's wisdom to plan factory output efficiently. That efficiency only came to light when I resigned from the company and Management had to replace me with two men, one just could not cope.

***"You (God) will guard him and keep him in perfect and constant peace whose mind (both its inclination and its character) is stayed on You, because he commits himself to You, leans on You and hopes confidently in You" (Isaiah 26:3 Amplified New Testament).***

Seven hundred years before Jesus arrived so dramatically in our world, Isaiah declared that one of His names would be **'GOD WITH US'** (60) translated from the Hebrew word **'IMMANUEL'**. Although risen from the dead and now holding the highest place in heaven, Jesus is still with us. Before ascending to His Father He said: ***"All authority has been given to Me in heaven and on earth. Go therefore and make disciples of all nations, baptising them in the name of the Father and of the Son and of the Holy Spirit, teaching them to observe all things I have commanded you; and lo, I AM WITH YOU ALWAYS, EVEN TO THE END OF THE AGE" (Matthew 28: 18-20 New King James Bible).***

We have in His Name and from His own lips the promise of His presence at all times. However, wanting always to re-assure us, God adds yet other powerful words: ***"I will not in any way fail you nor give you up nor leave you without support. I will not, I will not, I will not in any degree leave you helpless, nor forsake nor let you down—assuredly not" (Hebrews 13:5 Amplified New Testament). "If anyone loves Me, he will keep My word; and My Father will love him, and WE WILL COME TO HIM AND MAKE OUR HOME WITH HIM" (John 14:23 New King James Bible). "And you are in Him (Jesus Christ), made full and have come to fullness of life—In Christ you too are filled with the God-head: Father, Son and Holy Spirit, and reach full spiritual stature" (Colossians 2:10 Amplified New Testament).***

Let the significance of these amazing words grip your heart and mind until you are fully persuaded that you are never, ever out of God's presence. Don't try and understand how God; can be with you; make His home in you; give you His fullness. Just accept these life-changing truths and by faith begin to realise that His powerful presence is there with you. No matter where you are; at home, at work, at school, walking, shopping, driving a motor vehicle, riding a bicycle or whatever you are doing; exercising, resting, sleeping, eating, drinking, working, playing, there with you is your God. With these thoughts uppermost in your mind it is quite possible to discover within you a desire to shout—-Glory to God!

By now you should have re-ordered your life to keep all previous Holy Spirit revealed truths. Now add to your experience what is revealed in this chapter. The prime outcome of it all is to make sure you cultivate an awareness of God's presence at all times. By reason of this pleasant discipline your every day will be transformed from the natural into the supernatural.

Now turn your mind loose and imagine that you have by your side the physical person of the Lord Jesus and you are holding His hand. As you together negotiate the day you would not be afraid of anything. Your confidence would be one hundred per cent regarding any problem or danger facing you. Neither would you be silent, you would chatter away with your companion, ask Him lots of questions, listen to His advice, share with Him everything. He in turn would assure you of His love, provide answers to your questions, comfort, encourage and protect you. All in all you would be a different person.

OK! Now exchange your imagination for faith in God's word which has already been spoken to you.

Immediately reality comes into view—**JESUS IS WITH YOU**. Although you cannot see Him with your natural eyes, nor feel your hand in His but nevertheless He's there with you. Be like Moses of whom it is said, that he endured because he saw Him who is invisible (61). Your eye of faith, your spiritual eye, should be seeing God at all times. This calls for a faith-discipline that yields terrific dividends. Begin now to put it into practice by confessing to Jesus, out loud if possible your beliefs: You love me Lord!—-I'm special to You!—-You're always with me!—-You give me wisdom!—-I'm led by Your Spirit!—-I'm not of this world!—-I belong to you and therefore I refuse to take on board its stress—-I receive Your peace along with Your wisdom. Again I would stress that this is not to be in any way a mechanical utterance but a faith utterance and the truths you confess as you hear them will undergird your faith.

***"A calm and undisturbed mind and heart are the life and health of the body"*** (Proverbs 14:30 Amplified Bible). You can be busy, even extremely busy, totally engrossed in your daily activities whatever they may be but totally calm and undisturbed in mind and spirit. This being the outcome of working to God's agenda not your own or that which the world seeks to impose upon you. I'm not talking here of fulfilling any work schedule as such. Employers have a right to set this but having the right attitude and approach to it while drawing from God's resources all that's needed to satisfy Him and your work obligation. Let your faith make life a constant enjoyment of His presence and the application of His wisdom.

* **When busy generally the outward turmoil imposes itself on our inner being resulting in tension within. When God's presence is acknowledged and His wisdom applied the inner man enters God's rest (62) regardless of outward activity.**

* ***"The fear of the Lord is the beginning of wisdom, and the knowledge of the Holy One is understanding"*** **(Proverbs 9:10 New King James Bible). Worship and Wisdom cannot be separated.**

* **Some aspects of truth revealed can sometimes be difficult to understand. Apply an 'on hold' to whatever you cannot comprehend. Believe, apply and enjoy the benefits of what you can.**

**Bible references**

---

**55. Romans 12:2 Amplified New Testament**
**1 John 2:15-17 Amplified New Testament**
**Colossians 1:13 Amplified New Testament**

56. Colossians 3:1-17 The Message p502-503
57. Matthew 6:33 New King James Bible
58. 1 John 5:19 New King James Bible
59. James 1:5-7 Amplified New Testament
60. Matthew 1:23 and Isaiah 7:14 New King James Bible

61. Hebrews 11: 27 Amplified New Testament
62. Hebrews 4: 1-11 New King James Bible

# CHAPTER NINE

## IT'S GOOD TO LISTEN

Many Christians have a real mind-set whenever the word 'prayer' is mentioned. In the Christian community, prayer is a subject common to all and yet so little understood. Most concepts of prayer are fashioned from traditional religious culture instead of the Scriptures. From the Scriptures we gather that prayer, in its simplest form, is communication between a worshipper and the Living God. Yet it is far deeper than that, prayer is the communion of loving hearts, a growing dialogue between Father-God and His child.

Apart from the Living God all other gods (so called) are just idols who neither speak nor hear. Those who address them and possibly sacrifice to them neither hear or receive anything except perhaps some psychological satisfaction. However, to true believers, the Living God both speaks to His children and hears them. This wonderful truth establishes prayer as a dialogue, a faith-exercise in spiritual communications.

If faith is absent from prayer it will not be prayer at all but only a volume of words of no particular benefit other than perhaps some satisfaction gained because the pray-er thought that was all that prayer required. ***"He that comes to God must believe that He is, and that He is a rewarder of those who diligently seek Him" (Hebrews 11:6 New King James Bible).*** Faith is an absolute necessity for prayer to be meaningful. True prayer does not focus on the act of praying but on the person of God and His desires. This is re-enforced to us by the realisation that basically we do not know how to pray and when we acknowledge this and thrust ourselves upon Him then, ***"...the Holy Spirit comes to our aid and bears us up in our weakness; for we do not know what prayer to offer nor how to offer it worthily as we ought, but the Spirit Himself goes to meet our supplication and pleads in our behalf with unspeakable yearnings and groaning too deep for utterance. And He who searches the hearts of men knows what is the mind of the Spirit—- what His intent is—- because the Spirit intercedes and pleads (before God) in behalf of the saints according to and in harmony with God's will" (Romans 8:26-27 Amplified New Testament).***

Effective prayer is praying according to the will of God and that, of necessity, begets dialogue. To review prayer, in terms of non-answers or the way prayer is conducted, doesn't generally cross the mind of the pray-er. It is all too easy to accept that

God answers prayer in one of three ways, yes, no or wait. To believe this is to dismiss the possibility that time and energy are being wasted because of a wrong approach to prayer. Often prayer comprises a series of requests based on what we believe are needs but mostly they are wants. It is presumption to expect that God will automatically come in on our requests just because He is the source of all supply. Our God is not just a pair of ears, He speaks His will. He patiently waits for us to enquire of Him as to His desires appertaining to situations. Then having heard from Him and enlisting the help of the Holy Spirit, we will begin to pray His will into reality.

Perhaps you think that God would show His displeasure if one was to have a close look at the sum and substance of one's prayer-life, especially when answers do not materialise as anticipated. God is well able to handle all our questionings and respond with gracious instruction...*"**when you pray....**"* To be effective our prayers should anticipate answers based on assurances derived from God's word. Don't be afraid to examine your prayer-life with a desire to change it for a life of prayer because that is God's desire and intent.

A good conversationalist is first and foremost a good listener, listening comes before uttering a word. With this in mind let us realise that before we can pray effectively, we need to cultivate good listening habits. Our great Shepherd-Saviour said ***"My sheep hear My voice, and I know them, and they follow Me" (John 10:27 New King James Bible)***. Do you hear your Saviour's voice as a regular ongoing daily blessing? Many years ago I was complaining to Jesus that I did not hear His voice very often. His reply was very challenging and humbling because I did have prayer times each day. He said, **'it's because you don't listen!** I then re-arranged my life to bring about change. If you want to talk things over with God on a regular basis you must first cultivate a listening ear. The listening ear I am talking about has nothing to do with your natural hearing but is an inward ear, a spiritual perception, a sensitivity to hear God. How does this come about? God declares the answer; ***"...faith comes by hearing, and hearing by the word of God" (Romans 10:17 New King James Bible).*** Regular Bible reading and hearing from God are inseparable twins.

Every day all sorts of things clamour for attention, many of them bearing the legitimate stamp. The battle for the mind is on and our enemy never goes on holiday. In order to redeem time (63) we need divine wisdom to know what to eliminate from our lives to free our ears to hear God and free our eyes to see God. Real discipline is often called for in this exercise but so rewarding in its outcome. Our Father-God waits for His children to develop open hearing by following His instructions. We often raise our voices to gain attention or to emphasise something but not so our God. He always speaks quietly, gently but nevertheless powerfully and only sensitive ears will register His voice.

Our Lord Jesus gave some advice about hearing ***"Take heed WHAT you hear"*** and ***"...HOW you hear" (Mark 4:24 and Luke 8:18 New King James Bible).*** The implication being that there are times when we have to deliberately shut our ears and close our eyes, to what I call, lower-level media. Only as we do this are we able to hear God's voice. Perhaps at first call these words will not be acceptable because of the discipline involved. If that is so, then remember that flesh will always oppose spirit. Also consider that you are now living for Jesus and not for yourself. As the listening habit gets under way and increases, joy also increases along with a growing desire to please God in all you do. There are no short cuts to success here. Persist in getting familiar with God's word and your spiritual ear will become increasingly sensitive to hear His voice.

Now move from developing the listening habit to the faculty of speech. How does a baby learn to talk? First by hearing the sound of words, spoken largely by other members of his/her family. After a period of hearing (listening), a baby will begin to talk, initially only a few sounds leading to a word or two. Then words will develop into sentences until speech is established.

We follow the same pattern in learning to pray, first we listen and then we talk. Hearing God and keeping His Word will automatically guide us to pray according to His will...and then we will pray again....and pray again..... and joyfully continue in prayer. The more we listen—the more effective our praying will be. By the way, the word 'keep', regarding God's Word, includes hearing, believing, confessing and obeying it.

As born-again Believers we are encouraged to ***"Pray without ceasing" (1 Thessalonians 5:17 New King James Bible).*** Careful consideration of this exhortation in the light of previous revealed truth opens to us another aspect of prayer. That of being able to pray at all times wherever we are because of our circumstances, not regardless of them. God is available for us in this matter because He has planned it this way for us to achieve success in daily living. As we continue to consider the multiple events in our lives from a 'listen and live' perspective, so we will secure for ourselves the ongoing experience of living carefree.

As we appreciate the need to engage in constant dialogue with God, we will find this is in contrast to the pattern prayer known as the Lord's Prayer (64). This is the prayer that Jesus initially taught His disciples and also us by implication. Just prior to verbalising this pattern prayer, Jesus advised against lengthening prayer by repeating words, as this neither impresses His Father nor does it expedite answers. As you progressively discuss with God daily events in your life and apply His wisdom, you will move more and more into Kingdom living. However, in negotiating this prayer-pathway the question could easily arise; is there to be a constant repetition of the pattern prayer? The answer is, No! Of course not! You might then ask; why give this pattern prayer? especially as the prayer itself can actually be spoken in two minutes or less.

Now there appears to be a conflict here, on the one hand we have unceasing prayer and on the other, a two minute affair. How can these two aspects of prayer be reconciled? The answer is quite simple and lies in what could be termed 'lifestyle praying'. Lifestyle praying is exemplified by the way you deport yourself throughout each day together with your attitude to each situation as it arises, all in the light of the pattern prayer. Your life lived daily towards God in this way will be an expression of the words of the pattern prayer.

Acknowledging God as your Father registers you as a King's kid, so live each moment as becomes such a royal relationship. All you do and say should enhance His great name. Your attitude and words are to be at all times pleasant, positive and constructive. All those people whose lives you touch each day are to be blessed through you. The whole ethos of your life declaring— I honour God the King, whose I am and whose presence is with me.

As you put His word into practice, His Will will be done on the earth, especially in that piece of earth comprising you. The outworking of truth in all that you do and say, readily declares that God's purposes are your prime target in life. As you search for and apply God's wisdom into every situation and relationship, your life will become ever more pleasing to Him.

God wants you to excel in your work whether you are an employer or an employee. Either way the prime reason for you working is not to obtain money but the opportunity to seek God's Kingdom and His Righteousness (65). Therein lies the secret of success in carefree living. Seeking God's Kingdom does not mean wasting your employer's time by preaching the Gospel to your fellow-workers, the silent yet powerful

**witness of your life will do that. Working to please God will automatically satisfy everyone concerned and His promise to provide all necessary things needed by you for living will be honoured.**

**God, your supreme resource centre, does of course meet your need through your salary. If this is insufficient He has other ways and means of supplementing it. Your employer or whoever provides you with cash is God's agent to sustain you in life. As you discharge your responsibilities with a trusting attitude, God will take ample care of you. When His Kingdom and Righteousness is your priority, His priority is you.**

**Your life must reflect forgiveness towards others, refusing to take offence regardless of any adverse action or word directed against you. Forgiveness, which is a faith-action of the will, automatically assures deliverance from temptation and evil.**

The whole of your life lived daily in this way fully expresses the pattern prayer. Your life itself becomes a faith declaration which God continually honours. Of course, it is inaudible as far as human ears are concerned but those whose lives you touch and who see your commitment to excellence are left in no doubt that God controls your life (66). The essential part of lifestyle praying is dialogue with God that allows you to draw from His wisdom and then to apply it into each and any situation under discussion. The overall effect is dynamic.

*** Listening to God is essential to carefree living. Unless we hear Him we cannot live to please Him. A developing awareness of God's presence brings about a corresponding improvement in our dialogue with Him.**

*** Lifestyle praying doesn't remove the need for supplication, petition, intercession and thanksgiving in prayer.**

*** Lifestyle praying easily converts to lifestyle evangelism.**
***"Follow Me and I will make you fishers of men" (Matthew 4:19 New King James Bible)***

**Bible References**

---

**63. Ephesians 5:15-16 New King James Bible**
**64. Matthew 6:7-13 New King James Bible**
**65. Matthew 6:19-34 New King James Bible**
**66. Matthew 5:13-16 New King James Bible**

# CHAPTER 10

## NITTY GRITTY

As a rule, parents generally want the best for their children, a reflection of the Fatherhood of God from which all human fatherhood flows. God is by far the best authority and has all the answers on how to bring up children. Together with my wife, Dorothy, we must have posed dozens of questions to God concerning the 'how' of parenting our three daughters. His wisdom was never denied us but the application of it was sometimes hard. However, the outcome of applying God's methods was that our children became loving, caring, responsible daughters, who were and still are our greatest friends. They now, all happily married, seek God's wisdom in bringing up their children. For God's best to be enjoyed by His born-again children, He needs willing and obedient listeners in order for them to ***"grow up in every way and in all things into Christ" (Ephesians 4:15 Amplified New Testament).***

Before we became children of God, selfishness ruled and shaped our lives for many years. Although now 'in Christ', our character on display exhibits from time to time the fruit of those years.

Often and all too easily there comes to the fore; Irritability; petulance; self-consciousness; jealousy; ill-temper; downright anger; envy; selfishness; sarcasm; self-justification; judgmental criticism; along with pride manifested in its many forms. The list is by no means complete. We need to realise that God loves us far too much to leave us as we are. He brings our attention to the nitty gritty of our present 'character on display' mode. Like a good, responsible Father He desires that we, using the agency of the Holy Spirit, will get rid of those negative traits in our lives (67). As and when they go He replaces them with Christ-likeness. To achieve this He has an amazing, daring master-plan.

Children are often encouraged to excel by offering them incentives but the prize always comes after the achievement. Not so with God, He gives the prize of His Righteousness to us from the outset of our new life in Jesus. We start our spiritual childhood with this glorious gift. Because we may not realise the incredible value of God's gift, He gives us a command; ***"BE HOLY, FOR I AM HOLY" (1 Peter 1:15-16 New King James Bible).*** Our God expects us to learn to live to the standard of righteousness that is ours through faith in Christ Jesus.

God is gracious and takes a specific interest in each of our daily lives. Every single event, relationship, circumstance does not escape His all-seeing eye or attention. He is far from being a neglectful Father and quite aware of what is happening to you at any given moment. He is no stranger to your present circumstances. He has mightily encouraged you by already declaring His presence with and in you and given you many other promises. Here is yet another one which has a unique origin and all embracing. God first gave it to Abraham saying ***"Surely blessing I will bless you, and multiplying I will multiply you" (Genesis 22:17 New King James Bible).***

History would have relegated this double promise of God and other promises (68) to Abraham's natural descendants had it not been for New Testament revelation. There we are told that all who exercise faith toward God through Jesus Christ, are not only children of God but also children of Abraham (69). As children of God but also children of Abraham we inherit God's promises given to him and by faith can freely apply them to ourselves.

Immediately this truth bursts into our understanding, faith recognises its importance and significance. Why and what is God really saying? In essence God is saying; look my child, faith with patience gains My every promise. However, to dispel any lingering doubt and to give extra assurance that I will fulfil my promises, I give you this double promise that secures to you sufficiency for the present and a glorious hope for the future.

***"Christ...having become a curse for us...that the blessing of Abraham might come upon the Gentiles in Christ Jesus..." (Galatians 3:13-14 New King James Bible).*** The object of God in so blessing us is that we will be a blessing to others. H.G. Smyth embraces this theme as he poses the question; " Is your life a channel of blessing? Is it daily telling for Him? " (G). The Scripture readily makes plain that for anyone to daily live, walk and talk with the Living God is to be richly blessed.

God's blessing is now yours to share. The guarantee of it continuing until fullness is come being the presence of the Holy Spirit in your life. ***"In Him (Christ) we have obtained an inheritance...having believed, you were sealed with the Holy Spirit of promise, who is the guarantee of our inheritance..."*** (Ephesians 1:11-14 New King James Bible). What more can God do to assure you that in putting Him first in everything that comprises your life, He will see that you have no lack in any direction?

Consider well the background of the Abrahamic blessing culminating with this amazing, divine, double promise. As your heart is gripped with this new truth, use it as a prelude to yet another key scripture in Father's astounding plan to move you into stress-free living. ***"WE KNOW THAT ALL THINGS WORK TOGETHER FOR GOOD TO THOSE WHO LOVE GOD, TO THOSE WHO ARE THE CALLED ACCORDING TO HIS PURPOSE. FOR WHOM HE FOREKNEW, HE ALSO PREDESTINED TO BE CONFORMED TO THE IMAGE OF HIS SON" (Romans 8:28-29 New King James Bible).*** Once again, watch out for one of those mind-sets to surface as you hear this all too familiar Scripture and to exclude you from the grand parade.

The word 'purpose' indicates a purposeful plan, a proposed intention. In the economy of God, He intends that the 'All Things' that make up your life, each will work Christ-likeness in you. God's grace has established this unique, tailor-made plan whereby you can be changed into His likeness. However, nothing is going to change until by faith you embrace each incident comprising the 'all things' in your life. Your acceptance of this transforming truth is absolutely imperative. By your accepting this truth you pass another milestone in your faith-growth that ensures a positive outlook on anything and everything you encounter as you transact life.

By saying that God has planned the ‘all things’ in a person’s life, I am not meaning that He initiates vile sicknesses, accidents, relationship breakdowns, calamities and other monstrous happenings. No! God is not responsible for these but is acutely aware of them as and when they appear in this world and in a person’s life. Your life is an open plan before God including the minutest detail of your life (70). All of this is due to His foreknowledge. Foreknowledge does not necessarily mean the elimination of monstrous happenings in our world or in a person’s life. The good news is that God’s grace encapsulates each negative in such a way that in spite of the evil, good can come out of it for those who love God. He plans that the ‘all things’ in your life, both negative and positive, will through Him become the instruments of change in you.

Paul knew this by revelation and took a positive stance against every negative and turned it into experiential truth. It was he who by the Holy Spirit declared that all things work for good to those who are God-called. A careful study of his life proves the point that God was able to turn the most horrendous incidents in his life for good.

In the course of your day you encounter positive and negative experiences. You no doubt find it easier to cope with positives but what of those unexplained negatives? Some of them often quite perplexing. Perhaps you thought that you could never have a positive attitude toward them. However, it is now possible as you home in on the subject of 'all things'. God has declared that everything, yes everything, positive and negative can work for your benefit. It is usually the most difficult situations that contain the greatest lessons to be learned. As your faith accepts this, your circumstances will cease to be a source of complaint. Why? Because you now know that they are there in the purposes of God for you. Amazing Grace has set up these stepping stones for your personal transformation to Christ-likeness. Wonderful!

Your acceptance of 'all things' will promote an enquiring attitude that prompts dialogue with God. Your life being ordered by His wisdom means, He can clarify any and every situation that you encounter during your day if you but ask Him. In doing this He will highlight what it is in your life that displeases Him. Whatever emotion surfaces at any crisis point during each day is generally the old character-trait that God is wanting you to get rid of. Putting it another way, when you react badly to things in your life, God is wanting to remove every negative self-expression that surfaces but needs your willing co-operation. As and when the Holy Spirit puts His finger on the button either your pride will gloss over the negative self-expression and excuse it, or, humility will recognise that you need to lose it and agree with God that it has to go. ***"Therefore, brethren, we are debtors—not to the flesh, to live according to the flesh. For if you live according to the flesh you will die, but if by the Spirit you put to death the deeds of the body, you will live. For as many as are led by the Spirit of God, these are the sons of God" (Romans 8:12-14 New King James Bible).***

Whenever you exercise your will in agreement with what God wants to change in you, it is the Holy Spirit who does the work. You will find His gentleness makes it a painless affair. However, there can be at first a contention between your flesh, of which the old character-trait is a part, and the Spirit's desire to promote Christ-likeness in you. Our flesh does not easily give in but where faith agrees with the Spirit and yields, victory is assured (71).

When the Holy Spirit has dealt a death blow to some old character-trait, do not be surprised if you find yourself again in the same circumstances that previously brought out the flesh in you. This is part of the testing to prove whether your flesh is dead in that area. Eventually you will laugh at circumstances that previously would have produced a flesh expression. However, because some character-traits are deeply embedded you may suffer some lapses before final victory. Should this happen, whatever you do, don't give up. Defeat in a battle doesn't mean losing the war, persist and the Holy Spirit will patiently lead you to final victory. ***"Trust in the Lord with all your heart, and lean not on your own understanding; In all your ways acknowledge Him, and He shall direct your paths" (Proverbs 3:6 New King James Bible).***

In accepting God's wonderful plan that all things working for good, positive attitudes arise towards everything, including negative experiences. Negative experiences are those adverse situations that normally would give rise to anxiety, distress, fear, pain, etc. As and when these 'negatives' arise and no old traits are apparent, your acceptance of each situation without complaint promotes peace and patience leading to forbearance. Should there be no ready answer to any situation you find yourself in, don't doubt, don't hassle, just patiently put them 'on the table' before the Lord. Somewhere, sometime you'll be given an answer.

During our daily lives things can arise that can be quite challenging, even frightening. Every one of them is there to service and advance God's divine plan. When we understand this and make them work for us, we enter into His rest. God is fully aware of all the myriad incidents in our lives having planned good from each of them. His intense love utilises all, even enemy interference, as a means of accomplishing His mighty purposes in and through us, in and through you. How amazing that even before the enemy's enterprises are launched against us, God's grace has taken hold of each one (the enemy's worst) to ultimately turn it to good.

By our submission to Him, that which the enemy employs to frustrate God's purposes actually advances them. The 'all things' that flow into your life are golden opportunities to prove God's faithfulness in His care of you. Paul said, ***"I have learned how to be content in whatever state I am. I know how to be abased and live humbly in straightened circumstances, and I know also how to enjoy plenty and live in abundance. I have learned in any and all circumstances, the secret of facing every situation, whether well-fed or going hungry. I have strength for ALL THINGS in Christ Who empowers me—-I am ready for anything and equal to anything through Him who infuses inner strength into me (that is, I am self-***

***sufficient in Christ's sufficiency)" (Philippians 4:11-13 Amplified New Testament)***. We too learn in the school of 'all things'.

Over the years the Holy Spirit has revealed to the writer numerous personal character-traits, each indicative of the need for change. I well remember when still a shy young Christian, misgivings arising when prompted by the Holy Spirit to witness to a queue of people waiting to enter a cinema. I finally obeyed and only by doing so, proved that God was indeed with me (72). A long time ago my anger exploded during a particular incident, immediately the Holy Spirit challenged me regarding this self-expression because it did not work the praises of God (73). By yielding to Him then, He took control of this character-trait and keeps it 'under wraps'. Then there were incidents where pride surfaced in me and had to be dealt with. Gradually along the way other undesirable baggage has had to be jettisoned. Those occasions plus many others were in some ways painful but only because my flesh-resistance was strong, but when I yielded, Oh! the joy! As I continue travelling through life with my divine companion, He continues the refining process.

It is possible to fail to read circumstances aright when God is intent on changing some character-aspect of our lives. When we do fail He takes us on a circular tour back to the same point of challenge until we come to terms with it and submit. In any prevailing circumstance our request should always be for understanding otherwise we could find ourselves going around in circles.

Perhaps the biggest challenge Dorothy and I have had to face was when God indicated we should go and serve Him in Africa. At forty-six years of age with two daughters in their teens and the third about to enter them, my career in management established, to move to the unknown in Africa—well?? I am happy to say we agreed. Afterwards a pathway of many challenges opened up to us. We experienced several miracles before I set foot on African soil three years later. After four months there, Dorothy and our youngest daughter joined me in Zimbabwe, known then as Southern Rhodesia.

While there we launched a Christian Literature ministry that later embraced Relief and Relief projects. The whole focus being the salvation of the lost. Quite quickly the whole operation escalated. During our twenty one years there, we saw over 151,000 people saved and discipled for Jesus. On one occasion I was at Beira, Mozambique asking God to show me a property which we could use as a Base, in order to reach people there more effectively. He took me to a derelict building, part of which was actually in the sea at high tide. As I looked at this ghastly wreck I felt God say, 'Restore it and I'll help you'. Little did I realise just then the enormity of or the variety of help that I would need. Neither did it enter my mind the miraculous pathway God would lead us along to part occupation within two years. That pathway continued until final restoration, including complete furnishing of its twenty-four rooms, eventuated some five years later. During the restoration period everything needed, excepting hardwoods, had to be imported as there was absolutely nothing available locally. The whole experience was such that my faith grew and grew as daily God's promises materialised in the face of multiple, difficult and extraordinary situations.

There are many illustrations I could give, all of them arising from our life time walk with God, each of them combine to say that all things do work for our happiness if we let them. Divine planning presents us daily with many, many golden opportunities, most of them are for direct character change or opportunities to serve others. It is up to us whether we take advantage of these opportunities as and when they arise. Reviewing the 'all things' past and present in my life I continually rejoice with thanksgiving because they have been and are the means of releasing me into stress free living and personal transformation. I also rejoice in that God gave us the privilege of participating in Kingdom extension in all those won and discipled for Jesus.

***"Is there anyone around who can explain God? Anyone smart enough to tell Him what to do ? Anyone who has done Him such a huge favour that God has to ask His advice? Everything comes from Him; Everything happens through Him; Everything ends up in Him. Always glory! Always praise! Yes. Yes. Yes.***

***So here's what I want you to do, God helping you: Take your every day, ordinary life—your sleeping, eating, going to work, and walking around life—and place it before God as an offering. Embracing what God does for you is the best thing that you can do for Him. Don't become so well adjusted to your culture that you fit into it without even thinking. Instead, fix your attention on God. You'll be changed from the inside out. Readily recognise what He wants from you, and quickly respond to it. Unlike the culture around you, always dragging you down to its level of immaturity, God brings the best out of you, develops well-formed maturity in you" (Romans 11:34-36 and 12:1-3 The Message, page 388-9).***

* Whenever we exhibit old character-traits we deny the headship of Jesus. He said, if we deny Him before men He will deny us before His Father.

This is serious stuff and should motivate us to change.

* Holiness is the sum total of all that God is, His glorious presence makes holy. The more He indwells us the more holy we are.

* God's mercies provide the 'all things' in our lives, their utilisation brings change. Such simplicity is astonishing. God's power effected in and through us which puts Jesus on open display *"Grow in the grace and knowledge of our Lord and Saviour Jesus Christ"(2 Peter 3:18 New King James Bible).*

## Bible References

67. Ephesians 4:22-32 Amplified New Testament
Romans 8:13-14 Amplified New Testament
68. Genesis 12:1-3 New King James Bible
69. Hebrews 6:11-20 New King James Bible
Galatians 3:7-14 New King James Bible

**70. Psalm 139:13-16 New King James Bible**
**Job 23:10 New King James Bible**
**71. Romans 8:13-14 New King James Bible**
**Galatians 5:16-25 New King James Bible**
**72. 1 John 4:4 New King James Bible**
**73. James 1:20 Amplified New Testament**
**Colossians 3:8 Amplified New testament**

# CHAPTER ELEVEN

## THE 'G R' PRINCIPLE

We live in a fascinating, wonderful world. Whether we look through a telescope, microscope or whatever confronts our eyes, it is altogether marvellous. Everything in our giant universe speaks of the genius of our great Creator-God. The exception being the utter world chaos of environmental abuse and human suffering, the result of lawlessness. God has established multiple laws in His universe that embrace every area of life, whether physical or metaphysical. The latter is largely ignored by mankind with catastrophic results but for us who know God, the knowledge of and submission to His laws should be a priority quest.

At the core of carefree living are the laws of 'Giving and Receiving' with its sister, 'Sowing and Reaping', while not forgetting 'Use or Lose'. A born-again Christian has an awakened mind to these and other vital laws by accessing Scripture. Faith being the golden-key to operate within these and other laws to enjoy that quality of life God has planned for you—-no fears—no anxieties—no stress.

Medical doctors, physiotherapists will all advise the necessity of exercising limbs otherwise muscle-wastage occurs with crippling effect. Similarly God's gifts, and everybody has some, need to be used to avoid spiritual atrophy. The onus is on us to discover just what is ours in Christ and to use such gifts wisely. An exercise in itself that is an adventure.

Any farmer or gardener knows that the bottom line of reaping is sowing. After sowing at the right time, providing the ground and weather conditions are favourable, a harvest can be expected. Not all attribute the reaping of crops to God's faithfulness but because His laws are impartial He sends His rain, wind and sunshine to bless everyone alike.

In the spirit-realm we are sowing something all the time whether we realise it or not. The seeds or plants we sow are either good or otherwise depending on our emotional attitudes and speech. Whatever we sow will come back to us, negative for negative or positive for positive. Either is a matter of choice. ***"Don't be misled: No one makes a fool of God. What a person plants, he will harvest. The person who plants selfishness, ignoring the needs of others—ignoring God! - - harvests a crop of weeds. All he'll have to show for his life is weeds! But the one who plants in response to God, letting God's Spirit do the growth work in him, harvests a crop of real life,***

***eternal life. So let's not allow ourselves to get fatigued doing good. At the right time we will harvest a good crop if we don't give up, or quit.***

***Right now, therefore, every time we get the chance, let us work for the benefit of all, starting with the people closest to us in the community of faith" (Galatians 6:7-10 The Message, page 473).***

Many Christians impoverish themselves through a misunderstanding of the law of 'Giving and Receiving', yet all of God's benefits lie within it. I call this the 'GR' principle for obvious reasons. When I speak of poverty here I am largely excluding finances. It is quite surprising the mind-set of many Believers when the subject of 'Giving' is raised or taught. Mentally they close all access to their money as though finance was the only medium for generosity. Getting to grips with the 'GR' factor is a lovely subject for study and application because it not only embraces almost all human activity but leads to a rich, satisfying life.

A mother has first to give herself to eating and drinking the right things for her body to yield milk for her baby. Her reward, the deep satisfaction of suckling her child. A baby has to give its mouth and energy to suck mother's breast before receiving milk. A student has to give time and attention to his Instructor before gaining knowledge. A motorist has to give consent to the Highway Code and drive accordingly to receive safe travelling and so we could go on.

God abides within His laws and sets the pattern of giving when He gave us His only beloved Son. Jesus' life here while among us exemplified giving. Now that He is exalted high above all, He still gives the treasures of God's grace to those who also give. God wants us to no way come short in the act of giving. Also to do it with great joy for it carries the hallmark of His will and the whole ethos of heaven. ***"God loves it when the giver delights in the giving. God can pour on the blessings in astonishing ways so that you're ready for anything and everything, more than just ready to do what needs to be done. As one psalmist puts it, He (the giver) throws caution to the winds, giving to the needy in reckless abandon. His right-living and right-giving ways never run out, never wear out. This most generous God who gives seed to the farmer that becomes bread for your meals is more than extravagant with you. He gives you something you can then give away, which grows into full-formed lives, robust in God, wealthy in every way, so that you can be generous in every way, producing with us great praise to God" (2 Corinthians 9:8-11 The Message, pages 451-452).***

God encourages you to freely give out of what you have. Giving begins with yourself to God. Not just a one-off commitment but a regular daily exercise (74). Then the ongoing giving thanks to God in and for all things without exception (75). Forgiveness is to be freely given to all who offend or hurt you, remembering God's forgiveness of all your offences (76). If you are at fault in any way don't make excuses but humble yourself and apologise, first to God and then the person or persons involved. At times this will involve time and travel and a humbling of yourself but do not neglect this, it is vital to your release from care (77). Hospitality is another area in the orbit of giving (78). When all these are a part of your daily life, the Holy Spirit will bring to your attention other things to give such as time, energy, encouragement, friendship, finances, clean speech, honour, compassion, mercy, a listening ear, love and many, many more. The more you give so the more you will receive to give more.

The exciting unfolding of your life in God by applying truth will have increased your spiritual awareness. Giving time to listen means receiving heightened hearing. In the realm of those who give good things, receiving good things is guaranteed. As you sow your best for God into other lives, your harvest will be bountiful. The more time you give to knowing God, the sweeter the intimate sharing becomes with thanksgiving bubbling over.

In the context of loving intimate dialogue, God now says to you ***"Do not fret or have any anxiety about anything, but in every circumstance and in everything by prayer and petition (definite requests) with thanksgiving continue to make known your wants to God"(Philippians 4:6 Amplified New Testament).*** These few but far reaching words give great encouragement and challenge us to freely dialogue with God. Great comfort can also be derived from these words, that of knowing that your Father-God attentively cares for you enough to invite discussion with Him about the things in your life. Oh yes! God does care for you.

God cares for you! Here is another faith-challenge. The challenge is to immediately call upon God and confide in Him your fears, your worries, all the things that bug you, anything that makes you unhappy. Yes! Talk freely about any of the 'all things' in your life but don't forget to give thanks for every one of them, remembering the divine purpose of 'all things'. The sequel to your obedience to this gracious offer is absolutely dynamic, for God goes on to say, ***"And My peace which transcends all understanding, shall garrison and mount guard over your heart and mind in Christ Jesus" (Philippians 4:7 Amplified New Testament).***

God sets out in these two Scripture verses from the Philippian letter, the basic 'how' of entering into permanent stress free living. These two verses, backed by previously revealed and applied truth, allow you to freely give your worries, cares, fears to God. Consider well this gem of a promise with your faith in overdrive, because God says that for simply talking things over with Him, He'll lift your burden from off you as you render thanks. He will then replace that burden, regardless of whatever it may be, with His peace, a peace that will take control of your heart and mind. This is absolutely amazing and it all seems to good to be true but it's gloriously true...PURE HEAVENLY GOLD IS YOURS.... PEACE OF HEART AND MIND for your unwanted baggage.

Your present cares could well include the consequences of activities in your past which seriously encroach upon the present and trouble you. Also wounds sustained along the way that have never been healed and whenever remembered flip your emotions. Should that be so, here's what to do to find release. Firstly, let your mind and heart rest in the knowledge that your past life is totally forgiven by God. Any power it had over you is absolutely broken. You are now free from all condemnation. " ***Therefore (there is) now no condemnation-no adjudging guilty of wrong-for those who are in Christ Jesus, who live not after***

***the dictates of the flesh, but after the dictates of the Spirit. For the law of the Spirit of life (which is) in Christ Jesus (the law of our new being), has freed me from the law of sin and death" (Romans 8:1-2 Amplified New Testament).***

With this knowledge uppermost in your mind take pen and paper and tabulate every event that troubles you. Against each situation write the names of all the persons involved. The outcome of the exercise will be a list of all the people who have offended you in some way, plus those who have wounded you. Don't forget to add to your list all those to whom you possibly have done damage. Please be thorough and exhaustive.

With your list before you and no time restraints, move into a prayer session with the Lord. Share with Him each listed incident along with the people involved. Do this in detail even to reliving the past. Don't be surprised if there are tears and emotional disturbance but don't let this deter you from doing it. Alone with God, GIVE AND SPEAK FORGIVENESS towards each person who has offended or hurt you. Then pray for each one of them without exception. Desire good things for them and bless them in Jesus' name. Go through each situation on your list. Mention each person involved individually until everything is confessed and settled. In effect you will be giving to God all your cares and true to His promise you will receive His Peace.

Let me emphasise that this is not a mechanical exercise whereby you just say things and all is well. You engage in a deep spiritual exercise whereby faith releases to God every care, one by one. You do this with a total assurance that He is taking them from you and encapsulating you with His peace. In such peace you can rejoice always. ***"Casting the whole of your care—all your anxieties, all your worries, all your concerns, once and for all—on Him; for He cares about you affectionately, and cares about you watchfully" (1 Peter 5:7 Amplified New Testament).***

*** God abides within all the laws in this giant Universe. He guides us to discover and function within them, the sure way to maximise on life.**

*** God's ways are in stark contrast to man's. God's methods are; Lose to win—Reign by serving—Die to live—Give to gain. All in all our generosity serves to enrich us.**

*** *"The world of the generous gets larger and larger; the world of the stingy gets smaller and smaller. The one who blesses others is***

***abundantly blessed; those who help others are helped"(Proverbs 11:24 The Message, page 886).***

**** Giving is love in action. "This is how God showed his love for us: God sent his only Son into the world so we might live through him. This is the kind of love we are talking about— not that we once upon a time loved God, but that he loved us and sent his Son as a sacrifice to clear away our sins and the damage they've done to our relationship with God. My dear, dear friends, if God loved us like this, we certainly ought to love each other"(1 John 4:9-11 The Message, page 597).***

## Bible References

74. 2 Corinthians 8:5 New King James Bible Romans 12:1-2 Amplified New Testament
75. 1 Thessalonians 5:18 Amplified New Testament Ephesians 5:20 Amplified New Testament
76. Matthew 6: 14-15 and 18:22-35 New King James Bible
77. Matthew 5:23-24 New King James Bible
78. Romans 12:13 Amplified New Testament Hebrews 13:2 Amplified New Testament

# CHAPTER TWELVE

## NO HIGHER OCCUPATION

When treading the 'discovery and application' truth-trail we soon realise that the centre and circumference of all that comprises life, and our lives in particular, is the Living God. Our relationship with Him began an eternal love-match, ***"We love Him because He first loved us"(1 John 4:19 New King James Bible)***. Such love inspires worship, the act of giving adoring devotion and honour to the Godhead—-Father, Son and Holy Spirit. A delightful, ongoing, developing activity of faith working through love (79). The ultimate occupation which encapsulates all others.

***"I appeal to you therefore, brethren, and beg of you in view of (all) the mercies of God, to make a decisive dedication of your bodies—-presenting all your members and faculties—-as a living sacrifice, holy (devoted, consecrated) and well pleasing to God, which is your reasonable (rational, intelligent) service and spiritual worship" (Romans 12:1 Amplified New Testament).***

**Your reasonable service** because Jesus has redeemed you to God. All that comprises you, body, faculties, possessions, now belong to Him.

**Your spiritual worship** because love has no reservations and desires to please God. All the changes that took place in your yesterdays must be presented to God for use today and every day. Then with Him in control you will then express His presence wherever you go and to whomever you meet.

***"Now thanks be to God who always leads us in triumph in Christ, and through us diffuses the fragrance of His knowledge in every place. For we are to God the fragrance of Christ among those who are being saved and among those who are perishing........For it is the God who commanded light to shine out of darkness, who has shone in our hearts to give the light of the knowledge of the glory of God in the face of Jesus Christ. But we have this treasure in earthen vessels, that the excellence of the power may be of God and not of us" (2 Corinthians 2:14-15 and 4:6-7 New King James Bible).***

It is an open secret that the treasure of God's presence is in you. However, He remains hidden until your faith recognises He's there and yields to His Lordship. Seeing Him who is invisible brings about submission of your will in favour of His. Worship is putting God at the centre of things. The happy sequel to any action in your life that places

God at the centre is an experience of resurrection life. Desire is then awakened for more and more of this dynamic dimension to living.

In the pursuit of resurrection life you more and more realise how important your words and deeds are because they always affect people. The people who are involved in your daily life, whether spoken to or just onlookers, will either be conscious of the Christ in you or just you. When you determine that your actions and words will put the Christ in you on open display then you will find that He makes you attractively different. ***"Let your light so shine before men, that they may see your good works and glorify your Father in heaven" (Matthew 5:16 New King James Bible).***

Worship is not just confined to church gatherings or private devotions but is a valid, vital part of market place action. Your worship of God can only flow out of your love for Him. The more you get to know and experience His love for you, the greater and more intense your loving response. As a consequence your worship will begin to find expression in all the different areas of your life. Don't be deceived into believing that church-based praise and worship are synonymous with singing. Praise can be expressed in other ways such as thanksgiving or in giving a testimony of what God has done for you.

All church-based singing is not necessarily worship and at times can be void of praise. All praise, whether sung or expressed in other ways can be but a facet of worship. To be true to Scripture, praise in relationship to worship would be better understood as 'praise in worship'(80). Similarly there is also 'singing in worship', 'listening in worship', 'working in worship', 'giving in worship'. Worship being the ultimate energising factor of all action.

Anything you do for the glory of God, anything you do that expresses your love for God and is solely done for that purpose, is worship. Your obedience to His revealed will also generate worship. Jesus said, ***"God is Spirit, and those who worship Him must worship in spirit and truth" (John 4:24 New King James Bible).*** True worship flows from your spirit-man, your God conscious part and is expressed through your self-conscious part, your body-man. Worship is always faith's response to truth revealed and obeyed. As your love for God increases because of a developing intimacy with Him, so your worship will increasingly extend into a lifestyle.

***"Let the word of Christ dwell in you richly as you teach and admonish one another with all wisdom, and as you sing Psalms, hymns and***

***spiritual songs with gratitude in your hearts to God. And whatever you do, whether in word or deed, do it all in the name of the Lord Jesus, giving thanks to God the Father through Him.....Whatever you do, work at it with all your heart, as working for the Lord, not for men" (Colossians 3:16-17 and 23 New International Version Bible). "So then, whether you eat or drink, or whatever you may do, do all for the honour and glory of God" (1 Corinthians 10:31 Amplified New Testament).***

Scripture reveals that worship is not confined to any one activity in life but is to be all embracing as you honour God in everything. The sum total of where you go daily, what you do and say is the target area for your worship. How do you eat an elephant? The answer is, one bite at a time. How do you climb a mountain? The answer is, one step at a time. How do you live resurrection life? How do you live carefree, become holy? The answer is, by one faith experience at a time.

You have steadily covered ground since opting for a stress free life. Just as Israel gradually advanced to possess the God-given promised land, so it will be for you. God has planned your way and will gently guide and as you respond, then step by step progress is assured

* Worshipping God is not an onerous duty to perform but a spontaneous, enjoyable action arising out of love for Him. Faith working through love brings God into our 'now'. The outworking of this transforms us and our circumstances.

* Truth is always revealed by the Holy Spirit (81). As often as you take time to open yourself to truth and apply it when revealed, determines your progress in stress free living.

* Eating, travelling, listening, conversing, working, leisure, cooking, teaching, whatever, in fact everything that makes up your life. All these are target areas in which you can and should worship God. Through lifestyle worship your relationship with Him will flourish which cannot be hid from others.

## Bible References

79. Galatians 5:6 Amplified New Testament
80. Revelation 14:7 Amplified New Testament
81. John 16:13-15 New International Version Bible

# CHAPTER 13

## TAKING YOUR PLACE

Having implemented to some degree each truth shared in previous pages, you should now be enjoying a new lifestyle. That lifestyle giving ample opportunity for you to reign as a king each day. Your faith bringing you out from being underneath your circumstances to being on top. The joy of the Lord's presence constantly welling up from within. That in turn initiating thanksgiving to God for His overwhelming goodness to you. You are now a more positive person and fast learning how to live abundantly. All of heaven's resources are at your disposal to achieve this.

Having come this far in experiencing the abundant life syndrome, of living for God toward others, you're attractively different. You now possess an outward perspective as opposed to inward-focused living which branded your former life. Your positive approach to your 'today' lies in the experience of faith. You are ready for anything and can cope with everything for God is with you.

***"I have learned how to be content (satisfied to the point where I am not disturbed or disquieted) in whatever state I am. I know how***

***to be abased and live humbly in straitened circumstances, and I know also how to enjoy plenty and live in abundance. I have learned in any and all circumstances, the secret of facing every situation, whether well-fed or going hungry, having a sufficiency and to spare or going without and being in want. I have strength for all things in Christ Who empowers me—I am ready for anything and equal to anything through Him Who infuses inner strength into me, (that is, I am self-sufficient in Christ's sufficiency)" (Philippians 4:11-13 Amplified New Testament).***

In living for God toward people our primary focus is on fellow-believers and then others (82). When we excel in love toward our brothers and sisters in Christ, then those outside of Christ will confess that God is in us (83). All love-action toward those in Christ will be the prelude to love-action toward those outside of Him. This latter action being an extension of the former.

Your love of God will only find its greatest expression as you first serve those who comprise your local church. Each Believer being a vital part of the whole as it seeks to impact society around it. Literally, the Church in the market place, its God ordained position (84). Love for Christians who gather in other churches, of whom you are largely ignorant, is expressed by praying for them and their leaders.

Being a part of a local church and involved in its various Biblical expressions is an exciting faith-building experience. Of course responsibility devolves upon leadership and membership alike for its function. As children of God we are a family and a local church is the family home where God enjoys His family. ***"After they (Peter and John) were permitted to go, (the apostles) returned to their OWN COMPANY and told all that the chief priests and elders has said to them......Now the COMPANY OF BELIEVERS was of one heart and soul..." (Acts of the Apostles 4:23 and 32 Amplified New Testament).***

A true family home is where one is for all and all is for one, mutual responsibility under the headship of parents. Here, each finds sympathetic understanding and acceptance in growing up into Christ. The head of any particular home (local church) are the leaders. They under Christ's headship are responsible for the spiritual welfare of those led and are available for counsel when needed. ***"Remember your leaders, who spoke the word of God to you. Consider the outcome of their way of life and imitate their faith. Jesus Christ is the same yesterday and today and for ever" (Hebrews 13:7 New International Version Bible).***

A home where everyone takes and gives nothing will soon end in disaster but where everyone esteems and considers others, love and care will freely abound making it a haven of rest (85). In such fertile soil the growth of spiritual character in each member will be evident along with no shortage of new-born babes.

A local church is also a temple of God. ***"Do you not discern and understand that you are God's temple, and that God's Holy Spirit has His permanent dwelling in you—-to be at home in you collectively as a church and also individually? The temple of God is holy—sacred to Him—and that temple you the believing church and its individual believers are" (1 Corinthians 3:16-17 Amplified New Testament).***

Your local church is not the building but the people who know God and gather in it, you being among them. In this holy temple of the Lord each born-again person is a believer-priest. They minister to and for God in various ways while giving Him worship. This can be with singing, playing musical instruments, declaring His praises, praying, listening to His word. Also giving money, exercising spiritual gifts and a variety of other activities. God responds to each worshipper with blessings and encouraging revelations. The whole being, for each and everyone, necessary preparations for their market-place activity. Each Believer's service in worship always extending far beyond local church premises.

As a soldier of Jesus Christ (86) you are encouraged to protect and arm yourself as you engage the enemy(87) while seeking to win the community around you. The Lord Jesus is your Commander in Chief who imparts battle strategies and commands mainly through your Fellowship leaders. This then makes your local church a Command Outpost, a significant unit in local, national and world evangelism (88).

From local and other churches, soldiers (missionaries) are sent out and supported. A missionary is a sent one which makes all Believers missionaries whether operating locally or elsewhere. However, we generally think of missionaries as those who go to foreign lands to share the Gospel. Whether we're sent locally, nationally or internationally, as soldiers ***"..the weapons of our warfare are not physical (weapons of flesh and blood), but they are mighty before God for the overthrow and destruction of strongholds" (2 Corinthians 10:4 Amplified New Testament).*** You may well be asking, what are these weapons that in faith I must use?

From the Scriptures we understand that they are; **the Name of Jesus——the Blood of Jesus——the Word of God and our Praise of God.** The wisdom and strength to use these weapons effectively and to wear the God-given protective armour is through prayer and more prayer (89).

Each truth you have discovered and applied while reading this book, has been introduced to you in a particular order. No such order exists in practice. Each truth gained, together with any future revelation, take their place in your spiritual storehouse. From there to be again applied under the Holy Spirit's guidance depending on current situations you find yourself in. All in all applied faith to function daily in powerful Kingdom Living. In the never ending unfolding of God's grace you are a vital part of the solution to life. You now demonstrate this each day by living God's way, the way of Holiness.

As you take your stress free place in the church and in society, where are you going from here? It has to be to God Himself as He leads you on through experiences that constantly transform you into the likeness of His Son. So dear relative GO, GO. GO ....FOR THE SUPREME PRIZE for ***"the path of the just is like the shining sun, that shines ever brighter unto the perfect day" (Proverbs 4:18 New King James Bible).***

## Bible References

82. Romans 15:1-6 New King James Bible
83. John 17:20-23 The Message, P268
84. Matthew 5:14-16 New King James Bible
85. Hebrews 10:24 Amplified New Testament
86. 2 Timothy 2:3-4 New King James Bible
87. Ephesians 6:10-18 New International Version Bible
88. Acts of the Apostles 1:8 Amplified New Testament
89. Ephesians 6: 17-18 Amplified New Testament

# LIVING STRESS FREE

## Source of Quotations

A. Arthur Mee's book of 1,000 beautiful things. Hodder & Stoughton, London, UK.

B. Reprinted from Chamber's Biographical Dictionary © Chambers Harrap Ltd. UK. By kind permission by the publishers.

C. The Holiest of all by Andrew Murray. Fleming H. Revell Company, USA.

D. The Amazing Book of Bible Facts by Martin Manser Marshall/Pickering, UK.

E. Smith Wigglesworth. The Anointing of His Spirit W. Warner. Servant Publications, USA.

F. Smith Wigglesworth. as above

G. H.G. Smyth's Hymn, A Channel of Blessing contained in Redemption Hymnal Assemblies of God Publishing House, UK.